Treasures for the
CHRISTMAS TREE

101 Festive Ornaments to Make & Enjoy

Sterling Publishing Co., Inc.   New York
A STERLING/LARK BOOK

Art Director: Elaine Thompson
Photography: Evan Bracken
Production: Elaine Thompson
Illustrations: Charlie Covington

Photos page 17 and 61 by Bill Lee, Franklin, North Carolina

Library of Congress Cataloging-in-Publication Data
Taylor, Carol.
Treasures for the Christmas Tree: 101 festive ornaments to make
and enjoy / Carol Taylor.
    p. cm.
    "A Sterling/Lark book."
    Includes index.
    ISBN 0-8069-0806-8 Hardcover
    ISBN 1-4027-0133-0 Paperback
    1. Christmas decorations. 2. Christmas trees. I. Title.
TT900.C4T393   1994
745.594'12--dc20

                             94-13705
                                 CIP

10 9 8 7 6 5 4 3 2

A Sterling/Lark Book

Published by Sterling Publishing Company, Inc.
387 Park Avenue South, New York, NY 10016

Produced by Altamont Press, Inc.
67 Broadway, Asheville, NC 28801

© 1994 by Altamont Press

Distributed in Canada by Sterling Publishing
c/o Canadian Manda Group, One Atlantic Avenue, Suite 105
Toronto, Ontario, Canada M6K 3E7
Distributed in Great Britain and Europe by Chrysalis Books
64 Brewery Road, London N7 9NT, England
Distributed in Australia by Capricorn Link (Australia) Pty. Ltd.
P.O. Box 704, Windsor, NSW 2756, Australia

Sterling ISBN 0-8069-0806-8 Hardcover
        ISBN 1-4027-0133-0 Paperback

Contents

Contributing Designers

The Asheville Quilt Guild is a gathering of quilt makers who create projects large and small, including the occasional Christmas tree ornament. Page 32.

The Blue Ridge Basketmakers include 50 amateur and professional basketmakers and basket lovers from Western North Carolina. Page 78.

Julianne Bronder has 15 years' experience in the floral industry, both as a retail owner/manager and as a wholesale showroom designer. Currently, she works as a teacher, consultant, and designer of store displays. Pages 21, 72, 120.

Ellen Cantrell decorates 20 Christmas trees at Green River Plantation every year. An interior designer, Cantrell has spent seven years restoring the 1804 plantation house to its former grandeur. Located in Rutherfordton, North Carolina, Green River Plantation is open to the public. Pages 43, 86, 118.

Nona Donoho is an artist and illustrator who has worked extensively in the home furnishings industry. She also sculpts, makes beaded jewelry, and carves walking sticks. Page 119.

Elsie Fore and **Richard Pinkerton**, of Just for You Flowers in Asheville, North Carolina, enjoy creating arrangements that combine flowers and food. Page 98.

Marie-Helene Grabman, who learned the art of papercutting from her grandmother, has won several awards in juried shows. She is a member of the Guild of American Papercutters. Page 56.

Katherine Graham likes to paint useful objects—doors, tiles, flowerpots—since she believes that art should be a part of everyday life. She is primarily a poet. Page 20.

Clodine Hamilton is a gourd crafter with a stack of blue ribbons that her painted gourds have won in state and regional shows. She also works with other crafts, including an occasional okra pod. Pages 84, 106, 121 (driftwood).

June Hillyer is a weaver and teacher of weaving who became interested in temari balls when a Japanese exchange student spent a year with her family. With a few books in Japanese and some help from the exchange student's grandmother, Hillyer learned to make the string ornaments. Page 45.

Candee Hinman lives in a 19th-century farmhouse, which she has christened Whimsidippity Farm. When she isn't decorating every room in her house for Christmas, she is raising peacocks, swans, lambs, and English rabbits, along with miniature horses, goats, and chickens. Page 27.

Judy Horn teaches cornhusk crafts and makes cornhusk wreaths, dolls, and arrangements, which she sells at craft fairs and at her store, The Corn Husk Shoppe, in Weaverville, North Carolina. Pages 70, 94, 95.

Susan Kinney is a papermaker, a potter, a jeweler, and an interior designer. Pages 54, 55.

Suzanne Koppi is a special education teacher who turns to fabric and her sewing machine for relaxation and a creative outlet. Pages 28, 35, 44.

Aileen Lovelace crafts with seeds, cones, cornhusks, and other natural materials and markets her work at crafts fairs. Page 83.

Judy Mofield Mallow is an expert in the area of pine needle crafts. She markets her baskets, wreaths, and other works at craft fairs. Page 76.

Jan Morris designs and makes crafts from cones and cornhusks. Page 73.

Alyce Nadeau grows 200 different herbs for her business, Goldenrod Mountain Herbs, in Deep Gap, North Carolina, where she makes and markets wreaths,

arrangements, and other herbal and floral crafts. Pages 12, 13, 14, 15 (top), 16, 18, 24, 25, 103.

Morgan Owens-Celli is a wheat weaver from Long Beach, California. His work has been displayed at the Smithsonian Institution and at the White House in Washington, D.C. Page 91.

Beth Palmer is a painter and decorative artist who specializes in home accessories. Page 109.

Barbara Phillips teaches classes in working with cones and other natural materials. Page 93.

Marilyn Rehm learned to carve gourds from her father, a master carver. Her work ranges from large bowls carved from basketball gourds to small ornaments for the tree. Pages 74, 89 (birdhouses).

Mary Beth Ruby intended to become a potter but switched to versatile papier-mâché the day she discovered the instant material. She makes small objects for craft shops, large pieces for galleries, and one wall tree for a pet shop, where the store's cockatoos have insisted on roosting since the day it was installed. Pages 50, 52, 53.

Mimi Schleicher marbles on paper and fabric and is co-owner of Inklings in Asheville, North Carolina, where she sells all manner of marbled goods. She is co-author of *Marbled Designs* (Lark Books, 1993). Pages 41, 113.

Dottie Schulz is a decorative painter who likes to work on a variety of materials, including shells, wood, and papier-mâché. Pages 107, 121, 122.

Laura Sims markets her marbled paper, fabric, and objects through her business, Indigo Stone, in Asheville, North Carolina. She was a creative consultant for the book *Marbling Paper and Fabric* (Sterling, 1991). Pages 62, 67.

Diane Weaver is an artist, herbalist, and crafter. She is coauthor of *A Fireside Christmas* (Sterling, 1992) and author of *Painted Furniture* (Sterling, 1995). Pages 15 (bottom), 108.

Mary Wojeck grows all manner of gourds and makes them into a variety of projects by sawing, gluing, painting, and carving. Page 89 (gourd seed garland).

Ellen Zahorec is a mixed media studio artist specializing in handmade paper and collage. Her work has been shown internationally and is part of numerous private and corporate collections. Pages 23, 48 (left), 105 (bean balls), 110, 112, 114, 115, 116, 117.

And thanks to **Jan Davis** (page 11), **Will Albrecht** (page 126, crayon balls), and **Jennifer Wald** (page 96).

Special Thanks...

To **Aubrey Gibson**, florist, interior designer, and director of the annual Festival of Trees, a fund-raising event for the Mountain Area Hospice in Asheville, North Carolina. Gibson donates countless hours to the festival each year and was enormously helpful in the preparation of this book.

To **B. J. Crawford**, member of the Blue Ridge Basketmakers and co-owner of Earth Guild, a first-rate mail-order supplier of art and craft materials in Asheville, North Carolina. B. J. has taught basket-weaving techniques to countless numbers of people and was indispensable in developing the instructions for the basket tree on page 78.

To **Jill Chrigotis**, of the Asheville Quilt Guild, who has helped innumerable quilters unravel knotty problems and who was invaluable in developing the instructions for the Cathedral Windows ornaments on page 32.

To **Candee Hinman**, who generously allowed us the run of her splendid house for location photography.

Oh, Christmas Tree!

A Christmas tree is one of the best ideas anyone ever had. It sits joyfully in our winter-bound houses, green in a gray month, alive in the dead of winter, gleaming with light and color in a twilight season. Its sharp scent freshens our shuttered rooms, and underneath it are presents, small tokens of love.

Making ornaments for such a well-loved visitor is a pleasure. Sometimes "making" ornaments really means gathering them: finding a perfect lichen on a tree outside that will look splendid on the tree inside. Sometimes "making" means exactly that—using a few simple tools and readily available materials to create an ornament from scratch.

The ornaments in this book use a variety of materials and cover a wide range of moods and tastes. There are ornaments made from flowers and herbs. Others are fashioned from gourds, pinecones and pine needles, cornhusks, wheat, and straw. A few are made from foodstuffs. Others started out as scraps of fabric, ribbon, yarn, or string; some of these must be sewn, but most rely on fabric glue. Finally, there's a chapter on all that glitters—craft gems, minerals, hot glitter glue, foil, mylar, and plastic.

Scattered through the book are ideas for decorating miniature Christmas trees. Not every room needs a six-foot evergreen, but every room rejoices in a tiny tree. Miniature trees allow you to deck *all* the halls. (They also make welcome gifts).

When we make our own ornaments, we join centuries of tradition. We've been trimming the tree for a long, long time.

The Dark Night of the Solstice

From the beginning of recorded history, human beings have staged midwinter festivals. The occasion was the winter solstice, which we seem to have identified in our infancy, when the only astronomical instruments were eyesight and memory. Occurring on December 21, the solstice marks the longest night and the shortest day of the year in the northern hemisphere. From the middle of June until the middle of December, as the days became ever briefer and the nights ever longer, we shivered in ancient dread that the pattern was fixed, that we were on a relentless descent into the cold and the dark.

The solstice was the turning point. When we knew almost nothing else, we knew that after December 21 the days would grow longer and the nights shorter, the darkness would recede and the life-giving, soul-restoring light return.

Now that's a reason for a party.

Oh, Solstice Tree!

For at least 4,000 years, trees, especially evergreen trees, have been part of solstice celebrations. In Mesopotamia a 12-day festival encompassed the six days before and the six days after the solstice. The high point was a mock battle between the mythical Sun King and the forces of darkness. The Sun King won every year. As part of the general rejoicing, trees—the soldiers of the sun—were decorated and then burned.

The ancient Greeks staged a midwinter festival in honor of Zeus, draping evergreens and other trees with garlands of flowers and herbs. The Romans celebrated the Feast of the Unconquered Sun, which they called Saturnalia in honor of the god Saturn, and it was such a good party—feasting, gift giving, storytelling, and general revelry—that *saturnalia* remains a synonym for "orgy." During the season, private houses and public buildings were graced with evergreen trees and boughs, hung with candles, berries, and small trinkets that were eventually taken down and given as gifts.

In northern Europe, evergreens were even more central to solstice celebrations. The ancient Celts of Britain, Ireland, and France decorated evergreens and oaks with apples and mistletoe, as did the Teutons of Germany and Scandinavia. Norsemen simply dug the trees up, brought them inside, and burned circles of candles around the bases. They also burned an especially long-lasting log in honor of the god Yolnir, the light bearer—hence "Yule" log.

Solstice's End

Early Roman Christians did not celebrate Jesus's birth, even after Christianity became the established religion of the Roman empire in the fourth century. Never ones to turn down a good time, however, the Romans did continue to celebrate Saturnalia.

Troubled by these echoes of paganism, the church proclaimed December 25 to be the birth date of Jesus. Thus midwinter festivals became, not pagan occasions, but a time of Christian rejoicing.

Many solstice customs were incorporated directly into Christmas: feasting, gift giving, storytelling (carols, for example), and the lighting of fires and candles. When it came to evergreens, however, the church drew the line. Intimately identified with centuries of paganism, evergreens were strictly forbidden.

The ban was hard to enforce, especially in Northern Europe, where evergreens were abundant and especially revered. Ultimately, the church found a place for Christmas greenery.

Oh, Tannenbaum!

Legends about the origin of the Christmas tree abound. While they differ widely in the people and events they recount, most mention Germany as the place of origin. Happily enough, that's also where the historical evidence places it.

The ancestor of the Christmas tree probably appeared in medieval Paradise plays in Germany. Faced with an illiterate populace, the church enlisted actors to portray the Christian story in the public square. Every year on December 24, actors staged the fall of Adam and Eve and the redemption of Christ. The only stage prop was a tree hung with apples, representing the tree of knowledge in the Garden of Eden. (The church put a halt to the plays when actors began to spice up the dialogue with overblown speeches and ribald jokes.)

The earliest recorded Christmas trees appeared in Germany in the 16th century. By the 17th century travelers were reporting that some German parlors boasted fir trees decorated with paper roses, apples, wafers, gold foil, and sugar sweets. By the 18th century, visitors were describing a small tree for each child in the family, with presents of new clothing, dolls, and candy underneath.

Germans emigres carried the custom to the rest of the Christian world. Prince Albert, husband and consort of Queen Victoria and a German by birth, introduced the Christmas tree into the British royal household, and from there it was a short step to the rest of the kingdom. German teachers and professors in the United States set up Christmas trees for their children and helped to popularize the custom in America.

An old custom, a joyous custom, a custom that bridges nations and even, in the broadest sense, religions—the Christmas tree remains the centerpiece of our midwinter celebrations.

Tips and Techniques

To hang happily from the branches of your evergreen, an ornament needs to meet only a few requirements.

Size. Ornaments need to be in scale with the tree they decorate. Even the most gorgeously carved basketball gourd will look preposterous on anything except a 60-foot Douglas fir, and a thimble-sized ornament may look lost on a full-size tree. Consider how big your tree will be and design accordingly.

Weight. Evergreens have very flexible branches that bend under the weight of heavy snow and heavy ornaments. It takes very few ounces to make a branch as droopy as the post-Christmas blues.

Visibility. If you'd rather sell your grandmother into slavery than put up a Christmas tree that isn't green, avoid ornaments that use a lot of foliage or that are simply green. They'll disappear into the tree. If you have a white tree, perhaps one that's generously covered with artificial snow, greenery will show up nicely.

Density. While it's a matter of personal preference, many people think that a tree looks best when it's thoroughly decorated—when there are lots of decorations per square foot. Feel free to combine handcrafted ornaments with purchased ones and to fill in with additional materials (see "Fillers" below).

Tools and Materials

Making the ornaments in this book requires very few tools—a craft knife here, a pair of pliers there. Mostly you'll need to attach things to each other.

Adhesives are essential, and there are lots of good ones on the market—white craft glue, tacky glue, fabric glue, epoxy, and the venerable glue gun. (If you haven't noticed that glue sticks for glue guns now come in a variety of colors, with or without glitter, let us be the first to pass on the news.) The directions for each project suggest the adhesives that will work best.

Wire is a fine means of attachment—flexible green floral wire, available in just about every craft department, and the brass wire used in jewelry making and other crafts, available in most craft stores.

Floral tape—brown or green, depending on the materials—is also useful; it binds delicate materials without damaging them.

Base Balls

When you set out to make your own Christmas balls, you can choose from two widely available bases to support your materials. Both work well.

Polystyrene foam balls come in sizes ranging from huge to tiny. Lightweight, versatile, and invaluable, they have only two drawbacks. Hot glue melts them, requiring the use of a low-melt glue gun, and since they have nothing to attach a loop of ribbon to, some kind of hanger has to be constructed.

Equally useful are the inexpensive ornaments variously described as "satin" (they aren't) or "silk" (they aren't that, either). Wound with shiny thread, these balls are lightweight and inexpensive. They accept glue well, including hot glue, and they come with a built-in metal ring that's a fine place to attach a hanger.

Hangers

Functional as they are, those galvanized metal hangers we all grew up with don't do much for a handsome ornament. A simple loop of narrow ribbon in a complementary color makes an enormous difference in an ornament's attractiveness. Also useful are embroidery floss, dyed suede thong, and woven metallic cord.

Fillers

If you don't have the time or the inclination to make enough ornaments to fully decorate a tree, consider adding fillers—materials you can add to the tree that look terrific and require virtually no work.

Dried flowers look spectacular on a tree. Wire the stems into small bundles, then wire the bundles to the tree. Or, assuming a pet- and child-free house, just tuck the flowers among the branches. White baby's-breath is particularly versatile, but other, more unusual flowers, such as dried hydrangeas, can be striking.

Garlands frame ornaments beautifully, and a variety of materials can be draped around the tree—ribbon, grapevine, raffia, even the classic popcorn and cranberry. A "garland" of well-placed dried flowers encircling the tree can be wonderful.

Bows are fine fillers, especially considering the variety of ribbons to choose from: velvet, paper, mesh, net, cellophane, metallic, printed.

Packages—quick, easy, and broadly defined—can add a note of fun: popcorn or candy tied up in colored cellophane and hung on the tree, satin ornaments tied up in netting. Wrap tiny boxes in Christmasy giftwrap and hang them on the tree.

Transferring Patterns

Most of the patterns in this book are so simple that you probably won't bother to transfer them. Even those of us who are drawing-impaired can sketch a star or a heart or a hobby horse.

If you prefer to transfer the pattern directly, the simplest method is to find a photocopy machine. If the pattern is shown full size, simply photocopy it and cut it out. When half the pattern is shown, position it carefully as you photocopy it, leaving enough room on the photocopied page for the half not pictured. Then fold the photocopy along the dotted line of the pattern and cut through both thicknesses of paper, being careful not to cut through the fold.

If the pattern is shown less than full size, find a machine with an enlarging function. We've told you how much to enlarge the pattern to create a project exactly like the one shown. Of course, you can make it any size you choose.

Almost as simple is old reliable tracing paper. Simply trace the pattern and cut it out, following the instructions above for half patterns.

The cut paper ornaments on pages 57–60 have specific directions for transferring patterns.

Herbs &
Flowers

NATURE TREE

Some of the handsomest ornaments are already hanging in the trees outside. Look carefully in your backyard or along the roadside, and consider adding your finds to your own tree. Then fill in the empty spaces with materials from the craft store or from last summer's garden.

Materials
Grapevines or grapevine wreath bases, wasp nests, sumac heads, pinecones, tree lichens, Spanish moss, sprigs of German statice, red eucalyptus, wheat, dried hydrangea blossoms, long cinnamon sticks, brown paper ribbon, craft birds, decorative paper leaves, floral wire

1. If the grapevines are dry and difficult to bend, soak them in warm water overnight. Once they're pliable, spiral them around the tree and allow them to dry.
   If you can't find grapevines, you can buy vine wreath bases. Remove the hardware holding the bases together and soak the vines overnight in warm water. Once the vines are pliable, they'll be happy to uncoil.
2. Wire three or four cinnamon sticks together around the center, leaving long wire tails for attaching the bundle to the tree. Tie a bow of parchment-colored paper ribbon over the wire.
3. To make a tree topper, fashion a large, multi-loop bow of paper ribbon, leaving long streamers. Wire the bow together around the center, leaving long wire ends. Wire stalks of wheat and stems of red eucalyptus to the center of the bow. Tie another knot in the bow to hide the wires and fan out the foliage. Wire the decoration to the top of the tree.
4. Attach the remaining materials to the tree any way you can: with floral wire, hot glue, or just careful positioning.

❉ LUNARIA ORNAMENTS ❉

Pearly lunaria glimmer against a fresh green tree.

Materials

2-1/2-inch-diameter (6 cm) foam ball, about 36 lunaria membranes, tacky glue, glue gun, 3 dried mint leaves, 3 red globe amaranth, floral pin or other push pin, 17-inch (42 cm) length of cord

1. Place a thin film of tacky glue on the back of a lunaria membrane and mold it to the foam ball, holding it firmly until the glue is set.
2. Repeat with each lunaria until the ball is covered, leaving a bare spot about 1/2 inch (1 cm) in diameter at the top.
3. Tie the cord around the floral pin and push the pin into the bare spot; secure it to the ball with a little hot glue. Knot the ends of the cord to form a hanger.
4. Hot-glue the mint leaves in a trefoil shape around the hanger and glue the globe amaranth on top of the leaves.

Ancient Wisdom

Trees figure prominently in a great many religions, often as a source of enlightenment. In Scandinavian legend, the god Odin acquired his wisdom by drinking from the spring at the foot of a mighty ash, so huge that it connected the earth with heaven and hell. In the Old Testament story of the Garden of Eden, Eve was moved to eat the forbidden fruit when she saw that it came from "a tree to be desired to make one wise..."

❈ FLORAL POMANDERS AND WREATHS ❈

Rose-covered pomanders consume multitudes of tiny rosebuds, but the results are striking. Miniature vine wreaths can be decorated with a variety of small dried flowers.

Rose Pomanders

Materials
250 tiny rosebuds, foam ball 2-1/2 inches (6 cm) in diameter, glue gun, 7-inch (18 cm) length of ribbon 1/4 inch (6 mm) wide, 10-inch (25 cm) length of ribbon, floral pin or other push pin

1. For easier insertion, cut the rosebud stems on the diagonal.
2. Place a dot of hot glue on the foam ball and push a rose stem into the glue and into the ball.
3. Repeat until the ball is covered with roses, leaving a bare spot large enough for the floral pin.
4. Form the 7-inch length of ribbon into a loop and tie it to the pin. Shape the 10-inch ribbon into a bow and tie it to the end of the pin. Push the pin into the bare spot on the ball.

———— ❈ ————

Mini Wreath

Materials
Grapevine wreath base 3 inches (8 cm) in diameter, 4-inch (10 cm) piece of green floral wire, glue gun, 10 to 12 dried cat mint leaves, 4 red strawflowers, 4 dried rosebuds, 4 tiny clusters of white annual statice, 5 tiny yellow santolina flowers, 4 sprigs of lavender

1. Form the wire into a loop and attach it to the back of the wreath.
2. Hot-glue the dried materials to the base, beginning with the mint leaves.

✳ LAVENDER POTPOURRI ✳

Plastic potpourri balls have holes in both sides to allow the fragrance to escape.

Materials

3-inch-diameter (7 cm) plastic potpourri ball, 1/3 cup (80 ml) lavender flowers, 21-inch (52 cm) length of ribbon, 18-inch (45 cm) length of pearl garland, fine-gauge wire, glue gun, 4 dried mint leaves, 2 pink strawflowers, 2 purple globe amaranth, 2 sprigs pearly everlasting

1. Fill the potpourri ball half full with lavender flowers and close it securely.
2. Form the ribbon into a six-loop bow and wrap its center with wire.
3. Thread the pearl garland through the ball's plastic loop and tie it close to the loop. Position the bow on top of the loop, tie it on with the pearl garland, and knot the ends of the garland to form a hanger.
4. Hot-glue the other materials around the bow in the order listed.

The Origin of the Christmas Tree (Astronomy Version)

One clear December night, Martin Luther was making his way home through the forests of his native Germany. He stopped to admire the stars, which seemed to glitter in the branches of a magnificent evergreen. Entranced by such beauty, Luther went home, cut down a fir tree, set it in his house, and filled the branches with candles.

✻ ROSE-FILLED HEARTS ✻

If your ornaments are predominantly round, add a different shape to the tree.

Materials
Hollow, heart-shaped plastic ornament, 1/2 cup (120 ml) dried rose petals, narrow red metallic ribbon, glue gun, 2 dried rose leaves, 2 rosebuds, 2 tiny sprigs of white baby's-breath

1. Open the ornament and fill each half with dried rose petals. Close the ornament securely.
2. Thread a piece of ribbon through the clasp to serve as a hanger and knot it at the base.
3. Form a six-loop bow and tie it over the knot.

4. Hot-glue a rose leaf on each side of the heart and a rosebud to each leaf. Finish off with tiny sprigs of baby's-breath.

The Origin of the Christmas Tree (Forestry Version)

St. Boniface was an eighth-century English monk sent to convert the tribes of Germany to Christianity. One winter solstice, he happened upon a tribal chieftain about to sacrifice his son under a huge oak tree, to appease the gods and to bring back the light. Appalled, St. Boniface seized an axe and smote the oak one mighty blow. The oak split down the middle, revealing a small, perfect fir tree inside. The chieftain (and certainly the son) were converted on the spot.

✻ FLOWER-FILLED BALL ✻

The clear glass balls available at most Christmas stores are fine starting points for a crafter.

Materials
Glass ball, dried lavender, globe amaranth, statice, wired gold ribbon, glue gun

1. Remove the ornament cap and insert the flowers into the ball a sprig at a time, creating a pleasing arrangement.
2. Replace the cap, which will help hold the flowers in place.
3. Make a bow with long streamers and hot-glue it to the neck of the ornament.
4. As a finishing touch, hot-glue two tiny sprigs of statice and one of lavender to the top.

15

✕ WHITE-AND-SILVER TABLE TREE ✕

Dressed in snowy shades of flowers and foliage, this handsome table tree is resplendent with artemisia, pearly everlasting, yarrow, annual statice, and lamb's-ears. You can make it by hot-gluing any dried white flowers to an artificial green tree.

Materials

Artificial table tree about 2 feet (60 cm) tall with burlap-wrapped base, crocheted place mat or large doily, floral wire, 1-1/2 yards (1.4 m) of wired white ribbon 2 inches (5 cm) wide, large plastic bag, artemisia, pearly everlasting, white annual statice, white yarrow, lamb's-ears

1. Gather the crocheted place mat or doily around the base of the tree and secure it with floral wire or string.
2. Wrap a 24-inch (60 cm) length of ribbon around the base and tie it off. Make a bow from 30 inches (75 cm) of the ribbon and hot-glue it in place. Slip a large plastic bag over the finished base to protect it from glue.
3. Form small bouquets of three or four pieces of artemisia, fanning them out from the stems. Surround the stem ends with hot glue and insert the bouquets between the branches at the bottom of the tree. Working from bottom to top, place artemisia bouquets randomly around the tree, cutting the stems shorter as you move toward the top of the tree.
4. In a similar fashion, make bouquets of pearly everlasting, white yarrow, white annual statice, and lamb's-ears, and hot-glue them randomly around the tree.

Family Tree

All of earth's trees fall into three groups: the broad-leaves, such as oaks and maples; the palms; and the conifers. Ancient plants, conifers have a few defining characteristics. They have hard, narrow leaves known as needles or scales, depending on their shape; they produce cones (hence the term *conifer*) instead of true flowers; and almost all are evergreen.

Conifers grow around the world, most thickly in cold northern climates, where they circle the globe in a ribbon of forest that stretches across North America, Scandinavia, and Siberia. Farther to the south, conifers climb the slopes of cool mountains.

Unlike the broad-leaves, which drop their leaves during a few spectacular weeks in the fall, conifers shed their leaves a few at a time, continually replacing the ones that are lost. With their thick, tough, waxy skin, evergreen needles can survive the cold northern winters. Evergreens have also adapted to the huge snowfalls of the far north. The fir's downward-sloping branches and smooth, flexible leaves shed snow fairly efficiently; much of a heavy, two-foot (60 cm) snow will slide off the branches, rather than breaking them.

✺ HERB BALLS ✺

Herbs are beautiful enough (and fragrant enough) to merit a place on the most gorgeous evergreen. Note: Be sure you really like the penetrating scent of sassafras before you hang it on your tree.

Bay Leaf Ball

Materials

2-1/2-inch-diameter (6 cm) foam ball, about 18 bay leaves, straight pins, tacky glue, glue gun, raffia

1. Select a point on the ball to be the top, and use straight pins to fasten the tips of eight to 10 leaves near that point. With the tacky glue, glue the leaves to the ball one at a time, fanning them out over the ball and holding them firmly in place until they dry.
2. Glue additional leaves to the ball until it is covered.
3. Tie the ball up with raffia, forming the last 12 inches (30 cm) into a loop for hanging.
4. Make a six-loop raffia bow and hot-glue it to the top of the ball.

——— ✺ ———

Lavender Ball

Materials

2-inch-diameter (5 cm) foam ball, about 2/3 cup (160 ml) lavender petals, pie plate or flat dish, brush, tacky glue, raffia, 2 whole lavender blooms, glue gun

1. Place the lavender petals in the pie pan or flat dish.
2. Spread tacky glue onto a section of the foam ball. Press the glued section into the lavender petals and mold them to the ball with your hand.

3. Working section by section, continue in this fashion until the ball is covered.
4. When the glue is dry, tie up the ball with raffia, forming the last 12 inches (30 cm) into a loop for hanging.
5. Hot-glue several lavender blooms to the top of the ball.
6. Form a six-loop raffia bow and hot-glue it over the lavender stems.

——— ✺ ———

Sassafras

Materials

2-inch-diameter (5 cm) foam ball, about 2/3 cup (160 ml) sassafras chips (roots and bark), pie plate or flat dish, brush, tacky glue, raffia, glue gun

1. Place the sassafras chips in the pie plate or flat dish.
2. Spread tacky glue onto a section of the foam ball. Press the glued section into the sassafras chips and mold the chips to the ball with your hand.
3. Repeat with additional sections until the ball is covered with chips.
4. When the glue is dry, tie up the ball with raffia, forming the last 12 inches (30 cm) into a loop for hanging.
5. Make a six-loop raffia bow and hot-glue it to the top of the ball.

——— ✺ ———

Rose Petal Ball

Materials

3-inch-diameter (8 cm) foam ball, 1-1/3 cups (315 ml) dried rose petals, pie plate or flat dish, brush, tacky glue, raffia, glue gun

1. Place the rose petals in the flat dish or pie pan.
2. Spread tacky glue onto a section of the foam ball and press the glued section into the petals. Press the petals into the ball with your hand.
3. Repeat with additional sections until the ball is covered.
4. When the glue is dry, tie up the ball with raffia, forming a loop for hanging from the last 12 inches (30 cm).
5. Make a six-loop raffia bow and hot-glue it to the top of the ball.

The Origin of the Christmas Tree (Life Is Fair Version)

Once upon a time, a poor woodsman was making his way home on a bitter December night. He stumbled upon a small child—lost, hungry, and crying. Despite his own hunger, the woodsman took the child home to his tiny hovel and shared what meager bread he had. The next morning, the woodsman awoke to find a beautiful, shining tree outside his door, hung with all manner of good food and warm clothing. The hungry orphan had been the Christ Child in disguise.

✹ PAINTED POTS ✹

Terra cotta pots with black designs date back at least to ancient Greece. These distinctive ornaments look best when decorated with simple graphic designs—good news for most of us.

Materials
2-inch (5 cm) tall flowerpots; black, fine-tipped permanent marker; small pieces of floral foam (optional); dried flowers or grasses; floral wire

1. Sketch a few designs on paper first, until you find the ones that you like best.

2. Draw your designs on the pots with the permanent marker. If there are bold horizontal lines, make them first. For accuracy, measure down from the lip of the pot and place a few dots on those measurements, then connect the lines. Then fill in the details.

3. Fill the pots with the dried materials of your choice. (A small piece of floral foam in the bottom will make arranging easier.) Ours holds dried red strawflowers.

4. To hang each pot, wrap a piece of green floral wire just under the neck and twist the wire ends around a tree branch.

The Coming of the Christmas Tree (Cleveland Version)

In 1851 the Reverend Henry Schwan set up a Christmas tree in his church in Cleveland, Ohio. Outraged by such a blatant display of paganism, his congregation forced him to remove it. The pastor of another church, moved by his colleague's embarrassment, sent Reverend Schwan's congregation a huge, beautiful evergreen. Unwilling to spurn a Christmas gift (or ministerial solidarity), the congregation allowed the second tree to remain. The church has decorated a Christmas tree every year since then.

❋ SUNFLOWER TABLE TREE ❋

Fill in between the cheerful sunflowers with a variety of natural materials.

Materials

16-inch-tall (40 cm) artificial tree with burlap-wrapped base; glue gun; raffia; faux sunflowers 1-1/2 inches (4 cm) in diameter; green chenille stems; 3- to 4-inch (7 to 10 cm) pieces of straw; tiny cones, berries, or dried flowers; sprays of red berries; decorative pods; 3/16-inch-wide (5 mm) red velvet ribbon; fine-gauge floral wire; dried orange slices; sprigs of dried purple larkspur; sprigs of dried baby's-breath; 2 large, flat lichens

1. Make a raffia bow and hot-glue it to the base of the tree.
2. Wrap single strands of raffia around the tree as garlands, hot-gluing both ends to the branches.
3. Attach the sunflowers to the tree. If yours have plastic stems, remove the stems and hot-glue a short piece of green chenille stem to the back of the flower. Attach the flowers to the tree with the chenille stems.
4. Make the straw bundle ornaments, using the stems of wheat or large wild grasses. Lay six stalks together and wrap the bundle around the center with raffia. Hot-glue tiny cones, berries, and/ or dried flowers to the center. Tie the bundles onto the tree.
5. Hot-glue the sprays of berries and the decorative pods randomly around the tree.
6. Make two-loop bows with the red velvet ribbon and wire them to the tree.
7. Hot-glue the orange slices, larkspur, and baby's-breath randomly around the tree.
8. Hot-glue the lichens to the bottom of the tree.

❋ FLOWER TREE ❋

If you've ever wandered through the dried-flower section of a craft store and wished you could use everything you saw, here's your chance. This flower-loving tree is a natural for sunroom, sewing room, or bedroom.

Materials
Dried and/or silk flowers, floral wire, small gold Christmas balls

1. Make bouquets of the flowers and wire them together around the stems, leaving long wire tails. Vary the size and composition of the bouquets.
2. Wire the bouquets to the tree. In some cases, you'll be able simply to tuck the bouquets among the branches.

NATURE BUNDLES

❋

These collections of
natural evergreens are
striking on a white tree.

Materials
Evergreen sprays, dried weeds
and grasses, dried flowers, sprigs
of berries, tiny cones, metallic
spray paint, floral wire, florist
or parchment paper

1. Wander out into the woods (or
   into your backyard) and collect
   whatever materials catch your
   fancy. Use your imagination and
   be optimistic.
2. Spray-paint whatever looks in
   need of help, using gold and
   other metallic paints.
3. Arrange the materials in
   small sprays or bouquets and
   wire them together with
   floral wire. Add some tissue
   paper or parchment paper to
   finish off.

❋ HYDRANGEA WALL TREE ❋

If there's no floor or table space left for one more Christmas tree, move to the walls. Artificial wall trees can be dressed up for any room in the house.

Materials
Artificial wall tree about 30 inches (75 cm) tall with one flat side, green chenille stem, glue gun, sprigs of dried artemisia, dried hydrangea flowers, crested celosia flowers

1. To make a non-scratching hanger, form a green chenille craft stem into a loop and attach it to the back of the tree.
2. Straighten the wiry branches of the tree.
3. Hot-glue the artemisia around the sides of the tree.
4. Now hot-glue the hydrangea over the tree, filling it nearly full.
5. Finally, hot-glue crested celosia flowers randomly over the tree.

The Beauty of the Christmas Tree (Military Version)

The story goes like this. During the American Revolution, George Washington decided that Christmas night would be a fine time to attack a division of Hessians—professional German soldiers hired to fight for the British crown—who were encamped outside Trenton, New Jersey. Sure enough. The Hessians, completely engrossed in making merry around a candle-lit Christmas tree, failed to notice the approach of Washington's troops and were defeated.

While serious historians do not leap to confirm this bit of folklore, it is true at least that Hessian troops introduced candle-lit Christmas trees to the children of Newport, Rhode Island.

❈ ROSE TREE ❈

If your den doesn't have enough room for even a table-sized Christmas tree, tuck a tiny one into the bookshelves. If the tree is made of dried roses instead of live evergreens, it will need neither light nor water, and there will still be no mistaking its festive purpose.

Materials

9-inch-tall (22 cm) foam cone, glue gun, 3 cups (700 ml) dried rose petals, 1 dried rosebud about 1 inch (2.4 cm) long, 4 dried rosebuds about 1/2 inch (1.5 cm) long, raffia

1. Holding the foam cone by its tip, cover a small section at the base of the cone with hot glue. Press a handful of dried rose petals into the glued section. Press additional petals into the area until it is covered.
2. Working from bottom to top and section by section, cover the cone with petals. As you near the top, you'll need to hold the cone by the bottom.
3. Hot-glue the large rose to the top of the tree.
4. Wrap raffia around the base of the tree several times, make a six-loop raffia bow, and hot-glue it in place. Hot-glue the small rosebuds to the center of the bow.

Fabric Yarn, Buttons & Bows

❈ LACE ORNAMENTS ❈

If you long for a Victorian tree, you can create a beauty. Combine purchased ornaments—clip-on candle lights, glass balls and animals, spider webs, a Victorian doll wired to the top of the tree—with simple bows of 1-inch-wide (2.5 cm) lace ribbon. Stiffen the ribbon with fabric softener if necessary, and insert dried flowers into the knots. Add bunches of baby's-breath to fill in around the tree.

Lace Fans

Materials
10-inch (25 cm) length of 6-inch-wide (15 cm) lace ribbon, dried or silk flowers, floral wire, narrow ribbon

1. Pleat the lace end to end accordion style.
2. Wrap a piece of floral wire around the folded fan about 1 inch (2.5 cm) from one end, gathering the lace tightly. Allow the other end to open up, producing a fan shape.
3. Make a bow of the narrow ribbon.
4. Wire the bow to the bottom of the fan, along with a flower or two. Leave wire "tails" behind the fan to wire to the tree branches.

—— ❈ ——

Puffy Handkerchiefs

Materials
Lace handkerchief, potpourri, dried flowers, floral wire

1. Place a handful of potpourri (or even wadded tissue paper) in the center of the handkerchief and gather the edges up around it.
2. Insert a bouquet of dried flowers into the opening and tie up the bundle with string or floral wire.
3. Allow the edges of the handkerchief to fall down around the ornament to conceal the wire.
4. No need for a hanger; just tuck the ornament on top of a handy branch.

—— ❈ ——

Lace Doilies

Materials
Crocheted doily, plastic or glass flower, floral wire

1. Insert the flower through the center of the doily.
2. Wire the stem of the flower to the branches.

❈ CHRISTMAS ON THE FARM ❈

If you yearn for Christmas in the country, you'll think you've arrived every time you look at these ornaments—a herd of holsteins, a clothes-line full of long johns, some colorful quilts, and even packs left by a couple of hoboes, who stopped at the front gate to cadge a piece of pie. Only the quilts require sewing.

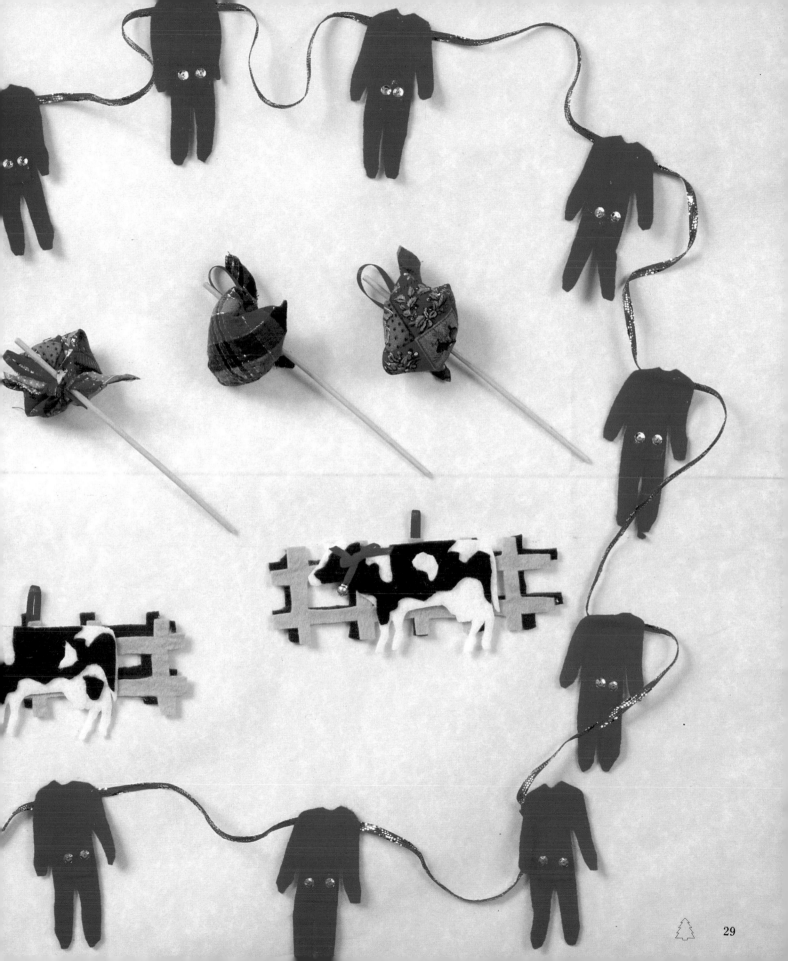

Long John Garland

Materials

(for 6 feet [1.8 m] of garland)
2 yards of ribbon 1/4 inch (6 mm) wide; 9- by 12-inch (22 X 30 cm) square of red felt; fabric glue; gold sequins

1. Cut nine long johns and nine seat flaps from the red felt.
2. Glue the flaps in the appropriate places. Glue sequins at the top corners, to resemble buttons. Allow to dry.
3. Glue one long john every 8 inches (20 cm) along the ribbon, attaching the underwear at about shoulder height.

Cow

Materials

9- x 12-inch (22 X 30 cm) squares of felt in white and black; squares of felt in brown and gold (optional); fabric glue; fabric stiffener; 8-inch (20 cm) length of narrow ribbon; 1/4-inch-diameter (6 mm) bell

1. Make one pattern for the cow, one pattern for the cow's black markings, and, if you plan to fence your herd, two fence patterns.
2. Cut the entire cow out of white felt; cut one piece of black felt in the shape of the cow's markings. If desired, cut one brown fence and one gold fence.
3. Glue the black pieces onto the white with the fabric glue. Allow to dry. Glue the gold fence onto the brown one, allowing some of the brown to show.
4. Stiffen each cow and fence with the fabric stiffener, following the manufacturer's instructions. Allow to dry.
5. String the bell on a 4-inch (10 cm) length of ribbon and tie around the cow's neck, adding a spiffy bow. Secure with a dab of glue.
6. If desired, glue the cow to the fence.
7. To make a hanger, glue a 4-inch loop of ribbon to the top center of the ornament.

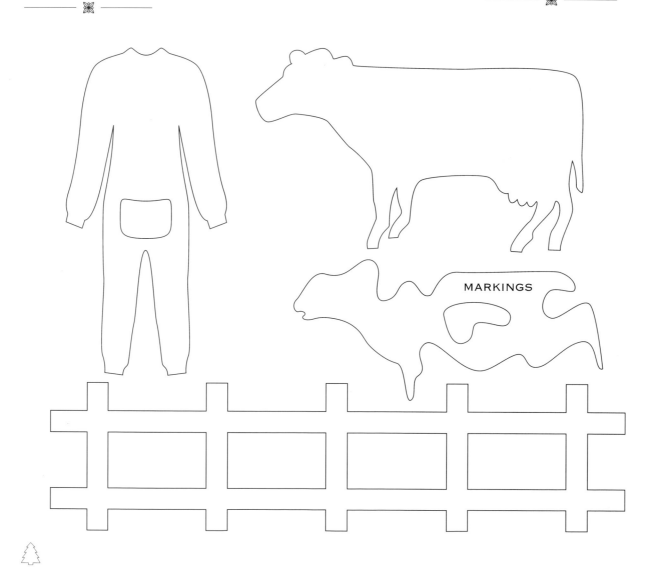

MARKINGS

Quilt

Materials (for 6 quilts)
About 1/4 yard (22 cm) of patchwork print fabric, 1/4 yard of complementary print or solid fabric, thin batting, 1 yard (90 cm) of ribbon 1/8 inch (3 mm) wide, sewing machine, large-eyed needle

1. For each quilt, cut out a rectangle of the quilt print and the complementary fabric, adding 1/4 inch (6 mm) seam allowances. The size of the ornaments will depend on the patchwork print; make them small enough to hang on the tree but large enough to include complete squares in the pattern.

2. With right sides together, sew a patchwork piece and a complementary piece together around the edges, leaving a 2-inch (5 cm) opening for turning.
3. Turn the quilts right side out and stuff with batting or a thin layer of fiberfill.
4. Stitch along all edges and along all pattern lines, creating a quilted look.
5. Thread the needle with a 4-inch (10 cm) piece of ribbon, pull the ribbon through a corner of the ornament, and knot the ends of the ribbon to form a hanger.

— ❈ —

Hobo Stick

Materials
6-inch (15 cm) length of dowel 1/8 or 1/4 inch (3 or 6 mm) in diameter, 6-inch square of fabric, 4-inch (10 cm) length of narrow ribbon, fabric glue, fiberfill or wadded paper

1. Form the ribbon into a loop and glue it 1-1/2 inches (4 cm) from one end of the dowel.
2. Place the fiberfill or wadded paper in the center of the fabric square.
3. Fold two opposite corners over the center, tucking one corner under the other. Fold the other two corners over the first two and tie them in a half knot.
4. Place a dot of glue on the knot. Place the dowel on the knot, so that the loop of ribbon sits, facing up, over the knot.
5. Tie the fabric ends over the dowel in a square knot. Secure with a final dot of glue.

And a Tip of the Stocking Cap, Too

Wilderness lovers, take heart: Virtually all of the 40 million Christmas trees Americans buy each year come from commercial tree farms, not from natural forests.

While a tree farm isn't as ecologically valuable as uncut wilderness, it's nothing to sneeze at, either. In this age of air pollution and acid rain, an industry that plants, re-plants, and cares for thousands of oxygen-producing, carbon-monoxide-consuming trees every year deserves a bit of environmental respect.

Cathedral Windows is a traditional quilt pattern, but you don't have to know how to quilt in order to make these stunning ornaments. Since the inset "windows" are only 1-1/2 inches (6 cm) square, you can use leftover scraps of various fabrics.

Materials

2 7-inch (17.5 cm) squares of gold lamé fabric, 2 1 1/2 inch (6 cm) squares of red-and-green fabric, matching thread, sewing machine, fiberfill, needle, gold cord

1. Fold a 7-inch square in half and stitch up the ends with a 1/4-inch (6 mm) seam. See Figure 1.

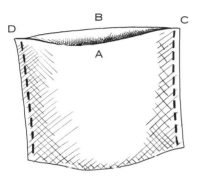

FIGURE 1

2. Pull outward at points A and B, so that C and D come together. Sew a 1/4-inch seam across the top, leaving a 2- or 3-inch (5 to 8 cm) opening in the center for turning. See Figure 2.

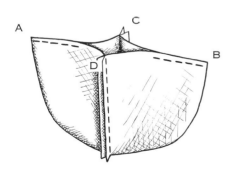

FIGURE 2

3. Turn the square right side out through the opening. Pull the corners out and press the square flat. Blindstitch the opening closed. See Figure 3.

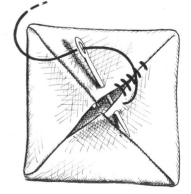

FIGURE 3

33

4. Fold the four corners so they meet in the center and press closed. The press marks will supply the seamlines. See Figure 4.

FIGURE 4

5. Place two folded squares back to back. Sew them together along two opposite creases. See Figure 5.

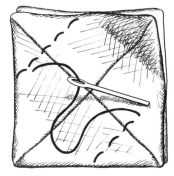

FIGURE 5

6. Fold the four corner flaps of each square toward the center and tack them together where they meet. See Figure 6.

FIGURE 6

7. Pull the two joined squares open, so that the seamline is in the center and the tacked flaps meet at each edge. You should see a diamond within a square. See Figure 7.

FIGURE 7

8. Center a small red-and-green fabric inset inside the diamond.

9. Fold the center of the loose edges of gold fabric down over the inset, creating a curved effect. See Figure 8. Whipstitch in place.

FIGURE 8

10. In the same fashion, sew a fabric inset to the other side of the ornament.

11. Whipstitch one open edge of the ornament closed. Stuff with fiberfill. Whipstitch the remaining edge closed.

12. Thread a needle with the gold cord. Bring the cord through one corner of the ornament and knot it, creating a loop for hanging.

Is It Fresh?

How can you spot a freshly cut tree, one that will look good and hold its needles through the holiday season?

Bend a single needle gently between your thumb and forefinger. If the needle is flexible, the tree is fresh. If the needle is brittle and breaks in two, the tree is aging rapidly. Run your hand down the branches. For most species, the needles should feel soft and flexible, not dry and stiff.

Lift the tree a few inches off the ground by its trunk and drop it back down. (If you're not up to hoisting a full-sized evergreen, shake a few branches briskly back and forth.) If needles shower onto the ground, the tree is advanced in years.

Finally, look for a tree that's locally grown; it may well be fresher than one that's been trucked across the country.

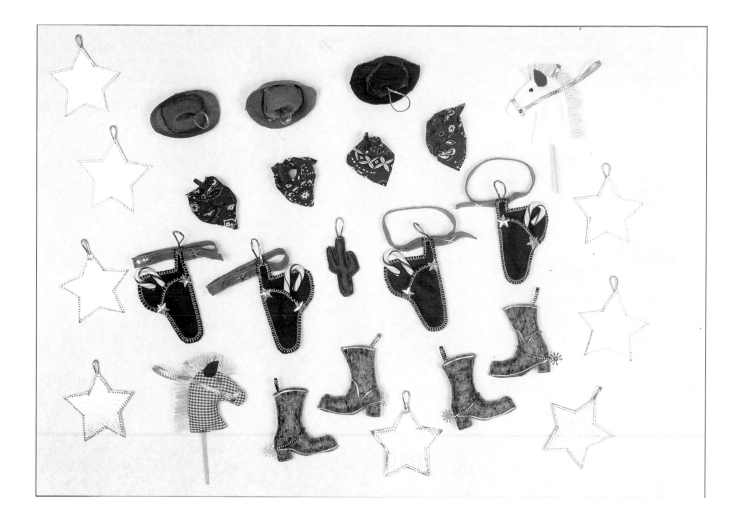

✺ WILD, WILD WEST ✺

If anyone in your household is still at the cowboy stage of development, you might wanna mosey on over to the old fabric drawer and make a tree that'll tickle their fantasies.

You can either photocopy the patterns at 200% or use them as guides to draw your own at any size you like.

Sheriff's Star

Materials (for 12 stars)
Poster board, 1/2 yard (45 cm) metallic fabric, glue stick, sewing machine with black thread, metallic braid to match fabric, matching sequins

1. Following the pattern, cut 12 stars from the poster board.
2. Cut pieces of fabric slightly larger than the stars. Apply the glue stick to the poster board and press a piece of fabric onto the star. Glue a second piece of fabric to the other side. Allow to dry.
3. Trim the fabric loosely around the stars.
4. Following the edge of the star, stitch through all layers about 1/8 inch (1.5 mm) from the edge of the poster board. Trim the fabric even with the paper.
5. Make a loop from the braid and glue it to one tip of the star. Glue a sequin over the glued end.

Cowboy Boots

Materials (for 6 boots)
9- by 12-inch (23 X 30 cm) piece of felt, decorative cord, snowflake sequin, fiberfill, sewing machine, fabric glue

1. Cut two pieces for each boot.
2. Wrong sides together, stitch around the boot close to the edge, leaving an opening for stuffing. Make a loop from a 1-1/2-inch (4 cm) piece of cord and stitch it into the seam at the top rear of the boot.
3. Stuff the boot to a medium fluff with fiberfill and machine stitch the opening closed.
4. Using the photo as a guide, glue braid to the boot. Glue the snowflake sequin to the heel as a spur.

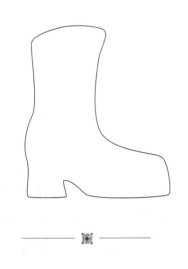

Bandanna Ornament

Materials (for 1 bandanna)
6-inch (15 cm) square of bandanna print material, fabric stiffener, narrow ribbon, fabric glue

1. Saturate the fabric with the stiffener, following the manufacturer's instructions.
2. Flatten the square. Then bring two opposite corners together to form a triangle.
3. Tie the corners into a loose knot and shape the projects with your fingers to look like a neckerchief. Allow to dry.
4. Make a loop of ribbon and glue it to the top fold of the bandanna.

Hobby Horse

Materials
Craft felt in two colors, fabric glue, 4-inch (10 cm) length of fringe, 14 inches (35 cm) of narrow ribbon, 4 sequins, fiberfill

1. Cut two horse heads from felt; cut two ears from a contrasting felt.
2. Glue the fringe around the top and back of one head piece, using the photo (or a horse) as a guide. Trim off the excess on the bottom.
3. Make a loop from a 3-inch ((4 cm) piece of ribbon and glue it to the crown of the head piece, on top of the fringe.
4. Glue the second head piece to the first, working near the edges and leaving the bottom open.
5. Glue the ears to opposite sides of the head.
6. Glue ribbon around the nose, beginning and ending at the position for the sequin (see the photo). Trim the end.
7. To make the harness, glue ribbon onto the head, beginning at the same spot as for the nose. Leave a loop of about 4 inches for a bridle.
8. Glue a sequin at the intersection of the nose ribbon and the harness.

9. Glue sequins in place for eyes.
10. Stuff head lightly and push the dowel into the stuffing. Glue the bottom edges together.

Cowboy Hats

Materials (for 2 hats)
5-inch (13 cm) circle of felt, fabric stiffener, fabric glue, shot glass or similar cylinder, 1 yard (90 cm) decorative braid or narrow ribbon

1. Cut the felt circle in half.
2. Bring the two corners of a semicircle together and, either by machine or by hand, sew the straight edges together from the corner to within 3/4 inch (2 cm) of the point. You should have a cone shape. Repeat with the other semicircle.

I Want That One, Daddy

The first known Christmas tree market appeared in 1531 on a street corner in the Alsatian town of Strasbourg. Every year since then, Christmas trees have been sold on that same corner. In the early days, townspeople were forbidden by law to have more than one tree, and it could be no more than "eight shoe lengths" tall.

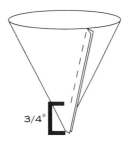

3/4"

3. Saturate one cone with fabric stiffener, following the manufacturer's instructions. Squeeze out the excess; the cone should be wet but not drippy.

4. Place the shot glass upside down on a piece of waxed paper and place the fabric cone over the bottom of the glass. Using the glass as a guide, shape the felt into a hat, using the photo (or a cowboy) as a guide. Turn up the bottom edges to make the brim, compress the hatband area, pull up on the crown, and crimp the top. There will be a hole in the "ditch" that runs along the crown. Continue to handle it as it dries to encourage it to retain its shape. When it seems stable, remove it from the glass and shape the second hat. If you're not pleased with a hat as it stiffens, saturate it again with fabric stiffener and start over.

5. When the hat is completely dry, glue the cord or ribbon around the crown, leaving two 2-inch (5 cm) ends to tie to one side. When the glue is dry, tie the two ends in a square knot and trim the ends.

6. To make a hanger, form an 8-inch ((20 cm) length of braid into a loop. Using a crochet hook or something similar, pull the loop through the hole in the hat, working from bottom to top. Tie the ends together into a knot under the hat and pull the knot up into the hat.

———— ✳ ————

Holsters

Materials
9- by 12-inch (23 X 30 cm) square of felt, sewing machine, fabric glue, 3 large star sequins, small candy cane

1. Cut one of each pattern piece from the felt. Also cut a piece of felt 1/2 inch by 6 inches (1.25 X 15 cm).

2. Using a decorative "blanket" stitch or a wide zigzag, stitch across the top of the front (smaller) piece.

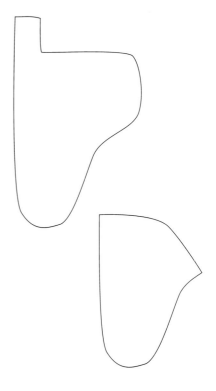

3. Place the small piece on top of the large one. Stitch around the edge of the two pieces.

4. Glue the sequins to the holster, using the photo as a guide.

5. Form the long piece of felt into a loop, overlapping the ends by 2 inches (5 cm). Stitch across the belt near the inside end. Glue sequins down the belt.

6. Glue the holster to the belt.

7. Glue a loop of braid to the back of the holster and place a candy cane in the pocket.

No, I Said That One, Daddy

In 1851 a farmer from the Catskill Mountains of upstate New York started the first known Christmas tree business in the United States. Mike Carr shipped fir trees by steamboat to New York City in early December and proceeded to sell them in Washington Market, near Greenwich Street.

A mere 30 years later, more than 600 tree sellers were competing for customers in Washington Market. A small tree sold for 10 cents, a large one for a quarter.

⌘ Country Charmer ⌘

The angels and fabric chains on this homey tree require no sewing. In fact, you can turn your best linen handkerchief into a Christmas angel, then untie it, unharmed, after the holidays are over. Small, unhemmed scraps of muslin also make delightfully down-home heavenly hosts. Small bunches of white baby's-breath tied up with raffia serve as fillers.

Angel With Raffia Wings

Materials

10- to 12-inch-square (25 to 30 cm) handkerchief, ball of polyester fiber-fill about 2 inches (5 cm) in diameter, heavy thread, raffia, 8-inch (20 cm) piece of medium-gauge floral wire

1. To make the head, fold one edge of the handkerchief 2-1/2 inches (6 cm) to one side. Place the fiberfill ball between the layers of fabric at the center. Tie thread tightly under the fiberfill (see Figure 1) in a secure knot. Trim the thread ends.

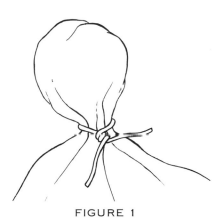

FIGURE 1

2. To make the arms, tie a top corner of the fabric into a knot close to the head (see Figure 2). Repeat for the opposite corner for the other arm.

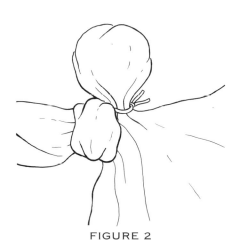

FIGURE 2

3. For the halo, wrap the floral wire with raffia. Bend it so that you have a loop in the center about 1-1/2 inches (4 cm) in diameter and a vertical "stand" in the back. Tie the halo to the angel's neck with the heavy thread.
4. Make a raffia bow to serve as wings, leaving long, graceful streamers, and tie the wings to the neck with heavy thread.
5. Tie a piece of jute around the neck, finishing with a two-loop bow.

Angel With Paper Wings

1. Make the angel by following Steps 1 through 3 above.
2. Cut a piece of beige paper ribbon about 5 inches (13 cm) long. If necessary, trim the ends to make smaller wings for smaller angels. Gather the ribbon in the center and tie it up with heavy thread. Tie the wings to the angel's neck.

Strung Hearts

Materials

5-inch (12 cm) squares of fabric (2 for each heart), matching thread, sewing machine, 18 inches (45 cm) of jute cord or other rustic-looking cord, large needle, fiberfill

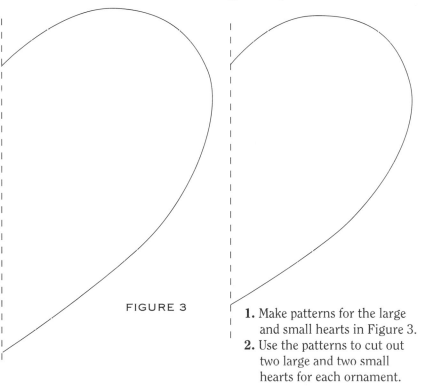

FIGURE 3

1. Make patterns for the large and small hearts in Figure 3.
2. Use the patterns to cut out two large and two small hearts for each ornament.

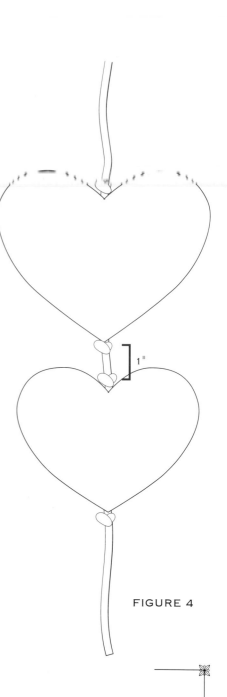

FIGURE 4

3. For each heart, place two same-sized pieces right sides together and sew around the pieces 1/4 inch (6 mm) from the edge, leaving a 1-inch (2.5 cm) opening.

4. Turn the heart right side out through the opening and stuff the heart with fiberfill. Sew the opening closed by hand.

5. Thread the large needle with the jute cord. Take the needle vertically through the center of each heart, knotting the jute just below each heart (see Figure 4) and tying a two-loop bow just above. Form the excess jute into a loop for hanging.

Fabric Chains

Materials
Bright printed fabrics, iron-on interfacing, fabric glue

1. Iron the interfacing to the wrong side of the fabric, following the manufacturer's instructions.

2. Cut the interfaced fabrics into strips about 3/4 inch (2 cm) wide and 6 inches (15 cm) long. Form them into chains (make sure the interfacing is on the inside), overlapping the ends and gluing them closed.

Care and Feeding

To extend the life of your *cut tree*, saw off the bottom inch (2.5 cm) of the trunk immediately, and stand the tree in a bucket of water away from wind, sun, and heat, until you're ready to decorate it. Fresh trees will drink a gallon of water a day, so invest in a tree stand with a large reservoir and check the water level daily.

If you're considering a dug-up *live tree* that you can re-plant after the holidays, keep in mind that they're extremely heavy; make sure someone in the household can lug one around. When shopping, look for a rootball that's large, intact, moist, and wrapped in burlap. Keep the tree in a cool place until it's time to decorate it. Once Christmas is over, plant it immediately if the ground isn't frozen hard. If it is, store the tree in a sheltered place with the rootball packed in straw until the next thaw. Spruces are the best candidates for live trees. They're the toughest of the common Christmas varieties and most likely to survive.

❊ GOD'S EYE ❊

An ancient design, a simple
God's-eye makes a good ornament
whether done in fine or heavy
yarn. The one shown uses varie-
gated yarn. You can also change
colors at any point in the con-
struction by tying a different color
yarn to the old color at the back of
the ornament. A God's-eye can be
made larger or smaller, depending
on your preference.

Materials
2 popsicle-type craft sticks or 2 pieces
of similar wood, glue, yarn

1. Cross the two pieces of wood in
   the center and glue them together. Allow to dry.
2. Hold the yarn behind the crossed
   wood so that the "tail" is in the
   lower left quadrant.
3. Bring the yarn to the front
   through the lower right quadrant
   and loop it over the right arm
   (see Figure 1).

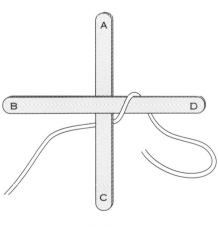

FIGURE 1

4. Bring the yarn around the right
   arm, then take it diagonally to
   the upper left quadrant (see
   Figure 2).

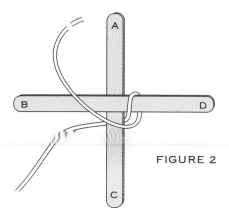

FIGURE 2

5. Turn the cross a quarter turn to the right.
6. Bring the yarn down behind and around the right arm, then diagonally to the upper left quadrant (see Figure 3).

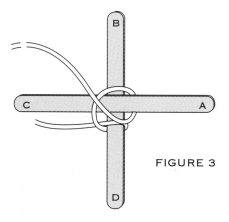

FIGURE 3

7. Turn the cross a quarter turn.
8. Continue this sequence ad infinitum. The movement is always down behind and around the right arm, diagonally up to the left, quarter turn of the cross. Each time you go around, try to lay the yarn right next to the yarn that's already there.
9. For several passes your yarn will form a giant X. Eventually, a diamond will appear in the center of the X.
10. When the God's-eye is the size you want (or when you're about to run out of sticks), glue the end to the back of the ornament.
11. Many people finish at this point, leaving the wooden ends extending from the yarn. If desired, you can add tassels to the ends. Just form a bundle of yarn 4 inches (10 cm) long, fold it in the center, and tie it around the "neck." Tie the tassel to one of the arms, shaggy end out. Make three more tassels for the remaining arms.

❊ TEDDY BEAR TREE ❊

If your daughter has a well-loved collection of bears, gather them together for a tree she will remember when childhood is long past. Some bears can be tucked into the branches, others will need to be wired respectfully to the tree. Fill in around the bears with lace fans (see fan-making instructions on page 27) and burgundy satin balls. And if the congregation isn't quite large enough, add some new members.

Materials
5- by 10-inch (13 X 25 cm) scrap of fabric, fiberfill, sewing machine, narrow ribbon, tapestry needle. For optional tutu: 2- by 72-inch (5 X 180 cm) piece of netting, fabric glue, extra ribbon

1. Cut two bears from the fabric.
2. Right sides together, sew the bears together, leaving a 1-inch (2.5 cm) opening for turning.
3. Turn the piece right side out and stuff with fiberfill. Stitch the opening closed.
4. If the bear wants a tutu, fold the strip of netting into about five layers and baste one long edge together. Gather the basted edge to match the bear's waist and tie off the gathering stitches. Straight stitch over the gathers several times for stability and trim the gathered edge evenly, within 1/8 inch (3 mm) of the stitching. Fit the skirt around the bear and tie it on securely. Add touches of fabric glue for security. Tie on a ribbon sash.
5. Thread ribbon through the tapestry needle and draw the ribbon through the back of the head and tie a 1-inch loop for hanging. Tie a piece of ribbon around the neck.

Safe Season

Go ahead and check your Christmas lights for shorts or frayed wires before you put them on the tree. (You have to replace all those dead bulbs anyhow.) And as delightful as it is to come home to a lit Christmas tree, it's the better part of valor to turn the lights off when the tree is home alone.

Finally, Dickensian fantasies notwithstanding, no completely sane person would attach candles to a Christmas tree *and then light them.* Consider 50 small fires on a tree that becomes better kindling with every day that passes—all inside your house. Christmas tree lights are available that look exactly (and safely) like miniature candles.

✖ TEMARI BALLS ✖

An ancient Japanese craft, temari balls are foam balls wrapped with thread—lots of thread. The designs are made with embroidery floss. The balls make stunning tree ornaments and are not difficult to do, but they require lots of patience.

Materials

Foam ball, serrated knife, jingle bell (optional), transparent tape, facial tissues, 250-yard (230 m) spool of sewing thread (for a foam ball that's 2-1/2-inches, or 6 cm, in diameter), paper, 4 skeins of 6-strand embroidery floss in various colors (or equivalent yardage of 5/2 perle cotton), metallic thread, serrated knife, measuring tape, tapestry needle size 18 to 24

Preparing the Ball

1. If you'd like a bell inside the ornament, cut the foam ball in half with the serrated knife and scoop out a cavity in each half that's about 3/4 inch (2 cm) deep. Place the bell in one of the cavities and tape the ball back together. If you don't want your ornament to jingle, skip this step.

2. Separate a facial tissue into two thin layers. Wrap one of the layers around the ball, to provide a soft base for wrapping and stitching. (For a larger ball, wrap two layers.)

3. Start to wrap the ball with the sewing thread, holding the tissue and the beginning of the thread in place with the first few loops. Continue to wind the thread around the ball in a random pattern until the ball is completely covered. When the ball is covered, thread a needle onto the end of the thread and secure the "tail" by passing the needle under several of the wrapping threads.

Post-Christmas Blues

Evergreen needles are slower to decompose than the leaves of broad-leaved trees, and they decay into a very acid humus. The acid leaf litter and the year-round shade in a thick coniferous forest make an inhospitable nursery for most seedlings. Light-filled openings between evergreen trees are usually occupied by acid-loving plants, such as ferns and toadstools.

God's-Eye Design

*(See the three blue balls
in the photo on page 45.)*

1. Cut three strips of paper about
1/4 inch (6 mm) wide and exactly
as long as the circumference of
the ball. Fold the strips in half
lengthwise, then in quarters.
Unfold the papers and mark a line
at each fold mark (see Figure 1).

2. Cross two paper strips at their
centers, so that the center marks
intersect, and pin the crossed
strips to the ball with a straight
pin. This will be the "North Pole"
of your ball. Bring the two strips
around the center of the ball and
pin them at the "South Pole" (see
Figure 2). If you need to use extra
pins temporarily to hold the
strips in place, feel free. Just
make sure there's one pin at the
North Pole and one at the South
Pole.

3. Circle the third strip of paper
around the ball at the "Equator,"
matching the various marks to be
sure it's centered between the
two poles. The strips should
divide the ball into eight segments: four above the equator
and four below (see Figure 3).

4. If you used extra pins to hold the
paper strips in place, remove all
but the ones at the intersections.
Tear the paper strips away.

5. Thread the needle with perle cotton in a color that contrasts with
the wrapping thread. This will be
your guide string.

6. Secure the guide string at the
north pole by slipping the needle
under a few wrapping threads,
then looping the string around
the North Pole pin. Take the
thread around the ball, securing
it at the South Pole and again at
the North Pole. Carry the thread
around the ball again, dividing
the ball into four segments.
Secure and cut the thread. Carry
a new guide thread around the

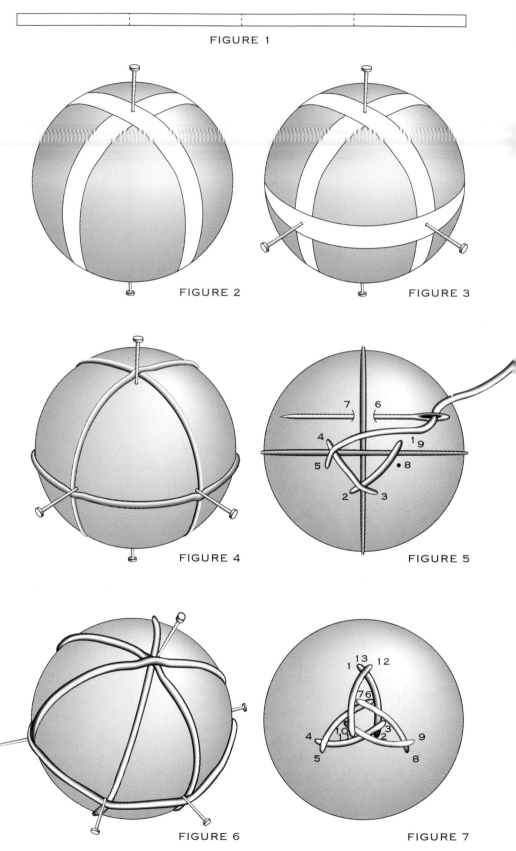

FIGURE 1

FIGURE 2

FIGURE 3

FIGURE 4

FIGURE 5

FIGURE 6

FIGURE 7

46

Equator, securing it at the pins. You now have eight segments (see Figure 4).

7. Thread the needle with the embroidery floss. Secure the floss by taking the needle under the wrapping threads about 1 inch (2.5 cm), exiting to the right of a guide string very close to the North Pole pin—Point 1 in Figure 5. Follow the diagram in Figure 5, turning the ball counterclockwise. Bring the thread over the next guide string (Point 2), then back under it and a few wrapping threads (Point 3), then over the next guide string (Point 4), then back under it and a few wrapping threads (Point 5), and so on, moving from guide string to guide string. Keep going around the ball counterclockwise. After a few rows, the threads will begin to form a square. Change colors of floss as you desire. Stop when you have reached halfway to the Equator.

8. Make additional God's-eyes at each intersection of the guide strings.

9. To make a hanger, loop a piece of floss or metallic thread through a handy guide string.

Six-Pointed Design
(See the pink ball in the photo.)

1. As for the God's-eye, use paper strips and straight pins to divide the ball into segments. This time, however, use three strips of paper to divide the ball into six vertical segments between the North and South poles. Add another strip for the Equator, and you have 12 segments—six above the Equator and six below.

2. Using embroidery floss, make a God's-eye at the North Pole, fol-lowing the previous instructions. Because of the additional guide strings, this God's-eye will have six sides instead of four. On the pink ball in the photo, the God's-eye is done in blue floss.

3. Work the three-pointed design by following the diagram in Figure 7. Again, you are securing the thread each time by going under the guide string and a few wrapping threads, then looping the floss back around the guide string.

4. Change colors of floss as desired. The three-pointed design will build from the inside lines to the outside lines. On the pink ball, for example, the first threads were the purple ones adjacent to the blue God's-eye. The second set were yellow, the third green, and so on.

⁂ Buttons and Bows ⁂

If your button box is overflowing with interesting specimens that have outlived the garments they once held together, combine your favorites with colorful ribbons and think of them as tree ornaments. A paper chain makes a good filler (see page 57 for instructions on making paper garlands).

Materials

Red, white, and gold ribbons; fine-gauge floral wire; buttons; glue gun, or needle plus very heavy thread

1. Form a two- to six-loop bow with the ribbon, leaving streamers about the length of the loops. Wire it around the center, leaving long wire ends for attaching to the tree.
2. If you don't want to use the button again, simply hot-glue it to the center of the bow, using as little glue as possible. If you want to salvage the button after Christmas, thread a 5-inch (13 cm) piece of thread onto the needle and, starting at the back, loop the thread through two of the button's holes. Remove the needle and tie the thread ends around the center of the bow.

   Note: For security, use the heaviest thread (or the thinnest cord) that will go through the button holes.

⁂ Button Balls ⁂

A bowl of old buttons at a flea market provided the inspiration and the raw materials for these ornaments.

Materials

Buttons, white satin balls, glue gun, glitter glue sticks, narrow ribbon

1. Apply hot glitter glue to a section of the ball and press in the buttons; the glue will be visible between the buttons, so choose a color that complements the buttons.
2. For the two-layered look on the balls at left and top, add a second layer of buttons, positioning them in the spaces left by the first layer and securing them with dollops of glitter glue.
3. Tie a piece of narrow ribbon in a loop for a hanger.

Paper

❈ PAPIER-MACHE ORNAMENTS ❈

Now that craft stores carry commercially prepared papier-mâché in jars, the formerly time-consuming medium is accessible to just about anybody. These handsome ornaments are just rolled, cut, and painted with acrylic paints. Be sure always to let each color of paint dry before you add details in another color on top of the first.

Making the Ornaments

Materials

Commercial papier-mâché, plastic wrap, rolling pin, pliable wire, wire cutters, plastic knives and/or plastic modeling tools, baking sheet, aluminum foil, acrylic gesso, acrylic paints, paintbrushes with medium and fine tips, acrylic sealer spray

1. Make the papier-mâché according to the package instructions.
2. Lay a sheet of plastic wrap on a level work surface. Place a piece of papier-mâché the size of a tennis ball on the plastic wrap. (That much papier-mâché will make six to eight ornaments). Cover it with another sheet of plastic wrap, and use a rolling pin to roll the pulp out to a thickness of about 1/4 inch (6 mm). Peel off the top layer of plastic wrap. Using a plastic knife or modeling tool, cut the desired shapes. With moistened fingers carefully lift the shapes onto a foil-covered baking sheet.
3. Cut the wire into 2-inch (5 cm) pieces, one for each ornament. Form a loop at the center of the wire by twisting the wire ends together (see Figure 1), and imbed the ends (not the loop itself) in the ornament. With damp fingers, smooth the pulp back into place and smooth any lumpy edges.
4. Let the ornaments air-dry for two days, turning them several times so that both sides dry evenly and the edges don't curl. If you're in a hurry, put the baking sheet into a 200°F (93°C) oven for 45 minutes.

FIGURE 1

Drying times may vary with the thickness of the ornaments, so check them frequently.

5. When the ornaments are dry, apply a coat of acrylic gesso (available in art supply stores and some craft shops), to give you a smooth, paintable surface that won't soak up enormous amounts of paint. Allow the gesso to dry.
6. Paint the ornaments and allow to dry.
7. When all paint has dried, spray the ornaments with acrylic sealer.

Parrots

These ornaments were decorated with metallic paint pens, which are easier to control than paints and paintbrushes. Acrylic paints, however, would work fine. Since real parrots wear plumage in colors that would put a Disney animator to shame, feel free to select any brilliant color you like for these birds. Your ornament will look more like a parrot if you sketch in the beak and eyes and define the neck by changing color.

Fruit Slices (page 52)

Apple: Paint one side of the slice and the edges bright red. Allow to dry. Paint the other side—the flesh—with white into which you've mixed a tiny bit of yellow. Add details of the stem, core, and seeds in brown.

Pear: The flesh is white with a bit more yellow than the apple. Add details of stem, core, and seeds with brown. Paint the other side and the edges of the ornament with bright green lightened with a little yellow.

Orange: Paint one side white. Carefully paint orange sections onto the white base, leaving a white rind, a small white circle in the center, and white lines between each section. Paint white lines radiating from the center in a random fashion and white seeds close to the center in some sections. Outline each seed in brown. Brush diluted yellow over the entire surface. Paint the edges and the other side of the ornament orange. Add dots of white and then brush with diluted yellow.

Lemon: Paint one side of the ornament white. Carefully add the yellow flesh, leaving a white rind and a white line down the center. Add white seeds close to the center line, then outline them in brown. Paint white lines radiating from the center line in a random fashion. Paint the edges and the other side yellow, then add dots of white.

Banana: Paint one side yellow mixed with white. Add a brown line along the center and small dots near this line for seeds.

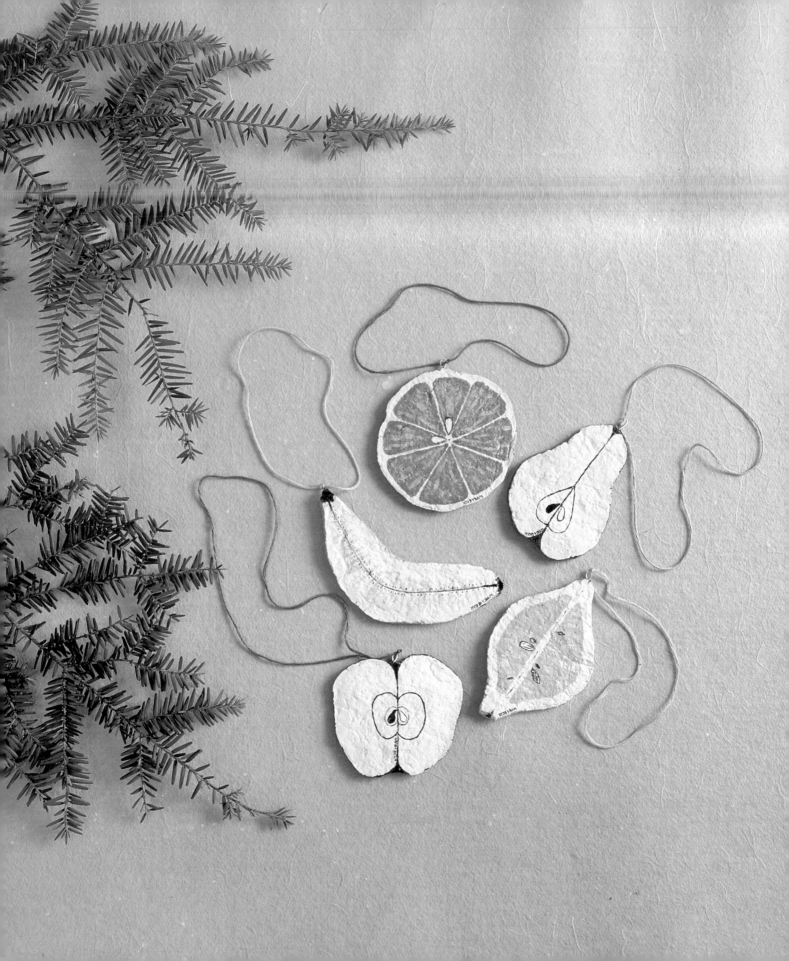

Fruit Bowl

Make the ornaments as described in Preparing the Ornaments, with an additional touch. For the strawberry and the bunch of grapes, shape small bits of papier-mâché into leaves and add them to the fruit when you make the ornaments. (Leaves can be added at any point—whether the fruit is wet or dry—but you'll have to wait for them to dry as well.)

Strawberry: Paint the berry red and its leaves dark green. Lightly brush pale green over the dark green on the leaves. Add bright yellow dots for the seeds.

Banana: Paint it bright yellow. Add brown lines and dots.

Grapes: Paint the fruit dark purple and the leaves dark green. Brush light green over the leaves. Use light purple and white to paint the individual grapes. Each grape needs a semicircular white highlight to look round.

Watermelon: Paint one side and the edges of the ornament light green. When that is dry, add stripes of dark green. Paint the flesh bright red, leaving a uniform border of white rind. Add black dots for seeds.

✳ HANDMADE PAPER ✳

Handmade paper is a beautiful substance, with an interesting texture and fascinating flecks of whatever raw materials went into it. Small scraps of it can be used to make arresting tree ornaments.

Materials
6- by 9-inch (15 by 23 cm) sheet of handmade paper or other thick, soft paper, foam ball 2 to 4 inches (5 to 10 cm) in diameter, white glue, brush, raffia

1. Tear the paper into irregular pieces about 1 or 2 inches square (2.5 or 5 cm).
2. Soak the pieces in a mixture of one-half glue and one-half water until damp.
3. Brush the surface of the ball with undiluted glue and press the damp pieces of paper onto the surface. The pieces should overlap; make sure there are no gaps.
4. Set the balls aside in a warm place to dry.
5. Tie the ball with raffia, dividing the ball into four vertical segments. Knot the ends to form a loop.

❊ PAPER WITH GOLD WIRE AND BEADS ❊

Gold-toned wire and off-white beads add festive touches
to handmade paper.

Materials

6- by 9-inch (15 by 23 cm) sheet of
handmade paper or other thick, soft
paper, foam ball 2 to 4 inches (5 to 10
cm) in diameter, white glue, brush,
20- to 28-gauge wire in gold or silver
color, needle the same diameter as
the wire, beads, straight pins

1. Tear the paper into irregular
   pieces about 1 or 2 inches
   square (2.5 or 5 cm).

2. Soak the pieces in a mixture of
   one-half glue and one-half water
   until damp.

3. Brush the surface of the ball with
   undiluted glue and press the
   damp pieces of paper onto the
   surface. The pieces should overlap; make sure there are no gaps.

4. Pierce the top of the ball with the
   needle. Insert the wire into and
   through the ball. Secure the wire
   end at the bottom of the ball by

   threading it through a bead,
   bending the wire back up over
   the bead, and twisting it around
   itself.

5. Wrap the other end of the wire
   around the ball in an irregular
   pattern, adding various beads as
   you go. Attach the wire to the
   ball as needed by inserting a
   straight pin into the ball and
   twisting the wire around it.

6. Set aside to dry in a warm place.

❋ CUT PAPER ORNAMENTS ❋

Ordinary paper becomes extraordinary when it's cut into festive shapes and hung on a Christmas tree. Ornaments can be cut from colored paper instead of white, if you prefer.

Materials

Medium-weight paper, sharp-pointed scissors, craft knife, string or decorative cord, artist's tape (or other easily removable tape), push pin

1. Copy the design from the book onto scratch paper and cut out the pattern. Cut out both the overall shape and all the interior spaces.
2. Fold in half the paper to be used for the ornament.
3. Place the pattern on the folded paper, positioning the dotted line on the fold.
4. Trace the pattern onto the paper. Be sure to include all interior openings.
5. Cut out the ornament, using the scissors for the outside and the craft knife for the interior spaces. *Do not cut through the fold.*
6. Repeat Steps 2 through 5, so that you have two identical cutout pieces of paper.
7. Place one cutout on top of the other, aligning them precisely. Tape the edges together with artist's tape.
8. If you want to decorate the ornament with pinpricks, do so now, punching a push pin through both layers of paper at regular intervals around the ornament. (The star and the heart shown in the photos are decorated with pinpricks.)
9. Lay a ruler along the center line and pencil light dots at 1/4-inch (6 mm) intervals. Make a small hole at each mark with a push pin.
10. Thread a needle with thread the same color as the paper. Don't knot the thread but do leave a 6-inch (15 cm) tail. Starting at the top, use the holes to sew the two pieces together with a running stitch (over, under, over, under). When you've taken the thread through the bottom hole, turn the ornament over and sew back up to the top. There will be thread between every two holes on both sides of the ornament.
11. Make a loop for hanging by knotting the thread ends at the top of the ornament.
12. Remove the tape and bend the four segments at right angles to each other.

——————— ❋ ———————

Garlands

Materials

Same as above

1. Copy the design from the book onto scratch paper and cut out the pattern. Cut out both the overall shape and all the interior spaces.
2. Accordion-fold a piece of paper. The number of layers of paper you end up with will be the number of angels or stars in your garland. Make sure the folded paper is as wide as you want the images to be.
3. Trace the pattern onto the folded paper.
4. Cut out the figure, being careful not to cut through the dotted lines on either side of the figure.
5. Unfold the garland and hang it on your tree.

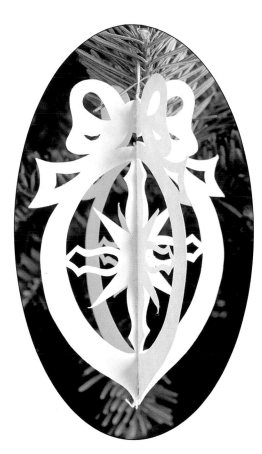

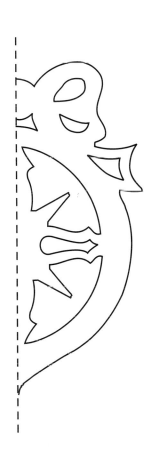

Why Evergreens Are Ever Green (Cherokee Version)

When all the trees on earth were newly made, the Great Spirit spoke to them. "I want you to stay awake and watch over the earth for seven nights," he said.

All the trees intended to obey. On the first night, everyone remained awake. The second night was harder, and just before dawn the sourwoods nodded off. On the third night, the trees whispered to each other in the wind to keep themselves awake, but even so, the dogwoods dozed. On the fourth night the maples slept, on the fifth night, the beeches, and, on the sixth night, even the oaks. After seven nights only a few stalwart trees remained awake: the pine, the spruce, the fir, the cedar, the holly, and the laurel.

The Great Spirit was very pleased. "You have great strength," he said, "great loyalty. You shall be, for all time, the guardians of the forest."

Ever since then, while other trees lose their leaves and sleep through the long, cold winter, the evergreens stay awake, keeping watch over the earth.

✻ KIMONOS ✻

These simple paper ornaments are made from handsome marbled paper, but you can make them out of any decorative paper.

Materials
Marbled paper (or other decorative paper), scissors, rubber cement, thread for hanger

1. Cut two pieces of paper 3 inches by 4-1/2 inches (7.5 x 11 cm). Cut them from two different papers. In a third paper, cut one piece of paper 1/4 inch wide (6 mm) and 12 inches long (30 cm).
2. To make the arms, fold one piece of paper in half along its length. On the side without the fold, cut the paper into a gentle curve (see Figure 1). Glue the wrong sides of the arms together.

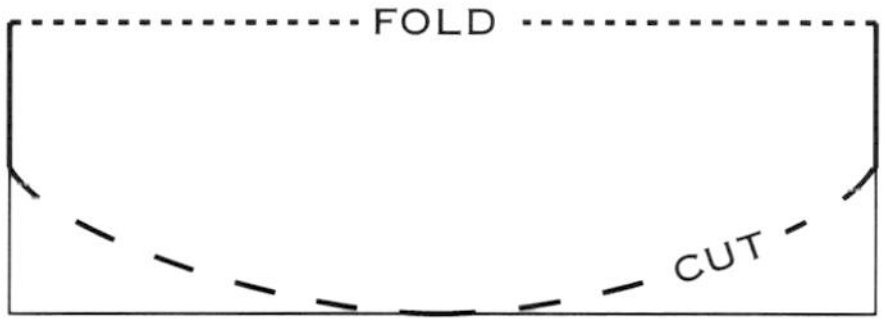

FIGURE 1

3. To make the body, fold the second piece of paper 3/4 inch (19 mm) from each long edge. The edges of the folded paper should meet in the center (see Figure 2).

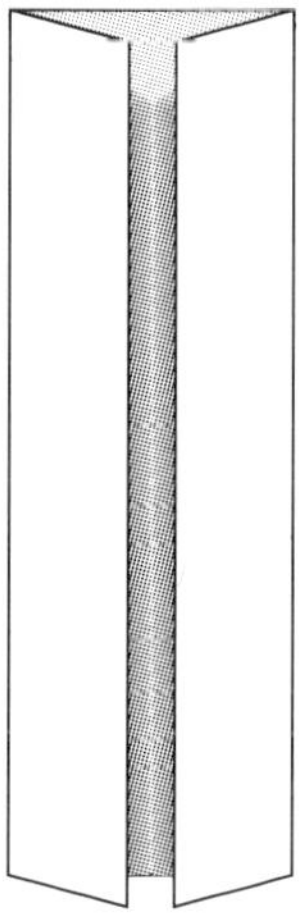

FIGURE 2

4. On one end of the body, cut along each fold 1-1/2 inches (4 cm). See Figure 3. Insert the arms into the slits. Glue the front of the body down flat.
5. Fold the long, narrow strip of paper in half, making a V-shaped fold (see Figure 4). Glue the folded strip to the front of the kimono, with just the V-shaped portion projecting above the kimono.
6. When the glue has dried, cut the kimono level at the bottom.
7. To make a hanger, loop a piece of thread through the V and knot the ends.

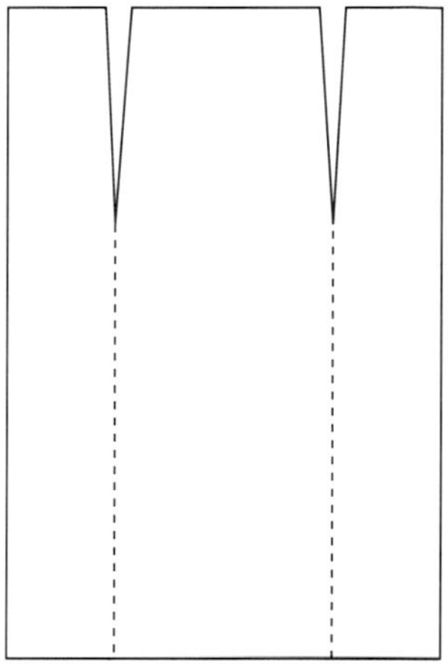

FIGURE 3

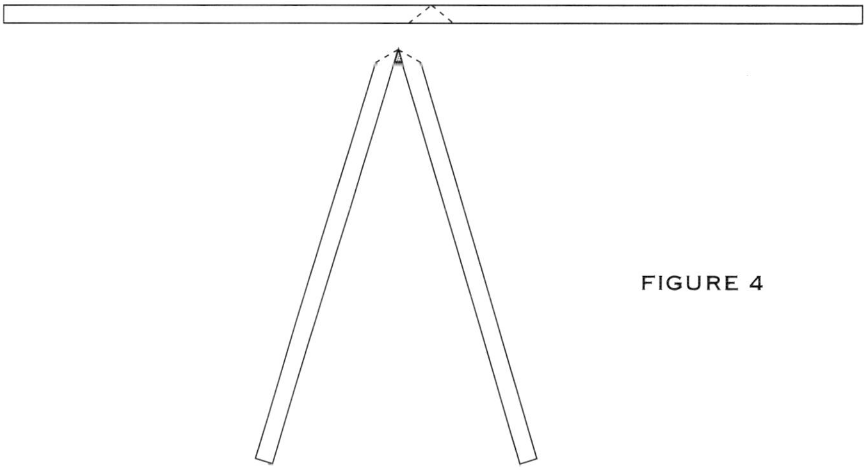

FIGURE 4

If Not a Christmas Tree...

Pines are also put to other, less seasonal uses. Able to grow on dry, sandy soils that would support few other crops, pines are probably the most important timber trees in the world and a major source of paper. In Germany and Sweden the needles are treated to remove the resin and soften the fibers; the resultant "forest wool" is woven into garments and stuffed into cushions and mattresses.

❈ PAPER DOILY TREE ❈

Inexpensive paper doilies serve as candleholders and tree toppers on this child-friendly tree. Bright cellophane lollipops and spicy gingerbread people add old-fashioned touches. When used as tree ornaments, gingerbread people need to be considerably hardier than when they're designed for eating. The recipe below makes some tough cookies to trim your tree.

Paper Doily Candleholders

Materials

Lacy paper doily, red "birthday" candle, white chenille craft stem, red and white ribbons 1/4 inch (6 mm) wide

1. Place the candle somewhat off center on the doily and gather the doily up around the bottom of the candle. The shorter side of the doily will be the front of the ornament, with the higher section in back.
2. Twist the chenille stem twice around the doily-wrapped candle, leaving a piece of stem free on each end.
3. Form a bow with the red and white ribbons and wrap the chenille stem ends around it. Use the remaining ends of the chenille stem to wire the ornament to the tree.

Gingerbread People

1 cup (235 g) margarine, softened
3/4 cup (135 g) firmly packed brown sugar
1/2 cup (90 g) granulated sugar
1/3 cup (80 ml) molasses
3/4 cup (175 ml) dark corn syrup
3 eggs
8-1/2 cups (1 kg) all-purpose flour
1 tablespoon baking soda
1 teaspoon salt
1 teaspoon *each* ground ginger, cloves, allspice, and cinnamon

Cream margarine and both sugars together. Add molasses, corn syrup, and eggs, and beat until smooth. Stir together the flour, baking soda, salt, and spices, and stir the dry mixture into the wet one. Divide the dough into two balls, cover with plastic wrap, and refrigerate two hours.

Preheat the oven to 350°F (176°C). Roll one ball of the chilled dough about 1/4 inch thick (6 mm), using a

floured rolling pin. With a cookie cutter, cut out as many gingerbread people as the size of your cutter will allow.

Transfer the cookies to a lightly greased baking sheet. Cut a hole for a hanger, using the end of a plastic drinking straw. Bake 10 to 12 minutes or until lightly browned. Place on wire rack to cool.

Thread a piece of narrow red ribbon through the hole to serve as a hanger, and tie a white ribbon bow around the neck.

Cellophane Lollipops

Materials

Foam ball 1 inch (2.5 cm) in diameter, craft pick, low-melt glue gun, colored cellophane, narrow ribbon

1. Glue the end of the craft pick to the center of the foam ball.
2. Wrap a piece of cellophane around the lollipop and tie it up with narrow ribbon.

Paper Doily Tree Topper

Materials

2 dozen paper doilies (or more or less, depending upon how large a tree you need to top), floral wire, narrow red ribbon, white glue

1. Gather a doily in the center, creating a cone with lace edges. Wire the doily around the center, leaving wire tails about 10 inches (25 cm) long.
2. Repeat with the remaining doilies.
3. Gather all the wire ends together, forming a huge "bouquet" of doilies. Insert the ends of the red ribbons down into the center of the bouquet. Twist the wires around each other.
4. To attach the topper to the tree, wrap the wires around a central upright spike.

The Selling of the Christmas Tree (Media Version)

In 1848 the *Illustrated London News* appeared with a charming drawing on the cover: Queen Victoria, Prince Albert (a German-born prince), and their many children gathered around a Christmas tree. The British public was enchanted, and the Christmas tree acquired a certain respectability.

Two years later, *Godey's Lady's Book*, an influential American periodical, printed the same drawing, tactfully erasing the queenly tiara and avoiding any mention of a royal family. Americans were delighted, and the Christmas tree gained wider currency.

❋ PAPER PINWHEELS ❋

Each pinwheel shown in the photo was made with two pieces of decorative paper: one marbled and one metallic. Any two sheets of pretty paper will work, as long as at least one of them has considerable body.

Materials

White glue (preferably one that remains flexible when it dries), 2 4-inch (10 cm) squares of decorative paper, waxed paper, ice pick, scissors, round-nosed jewelry pliers (or needle-nosed pliers), 2-inch (5 cm) length of 20-gauge jewelry wire (or other heavy-gauge wire), 2 small beads

1. Wrong sides together, glue the decorative papers together. Sandwich them between two sheets of waxed paper and weigh them down with a large, heavy book until dry.
2. Cut the glued papers into a 3-1/2-inch (9 cm) square.
3. Pencil a pale line diagonally between each set of opposite corners.
4. With an ice pick or similar tool, punch a hole where the two lines intersect.
5. On the left side of each quadrant, punch a small hole 1/8 inch (1.5 cm) from the point (see Figure 1).
6. Starting at the edges of the square, cut along each diagonal line, stopping 1/4 inch (6 mm) from the center.
7. With the pliers, bend one end of the wire into a closed loop.
8. Slip a small bead over the other end of the wire until it rests on the loop.
9. Slip the wire through the center hole in the square, going from the paper you want on the outside of the pinwheel to the paper you want on the inside.
10. Bring one corner of the paper toward the center and insert the wire through the hole. Bring the next adjacent corner to the center, then the next, then the last one, inserting the wire in each hole (see Figure 2).
11. Add the other bead to the wire.
12. Compress the center of the pinwheel and clip the wire about 3/8 inch (1 cm) from the top bead. Use the pliers to bend the wire end into a loop.
13. To form a hanger, punch a small hole in one wing tip, thread a piece of colored string through the hole, and knot the ends.

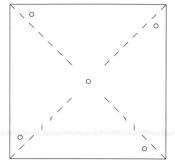

FIGURE 1

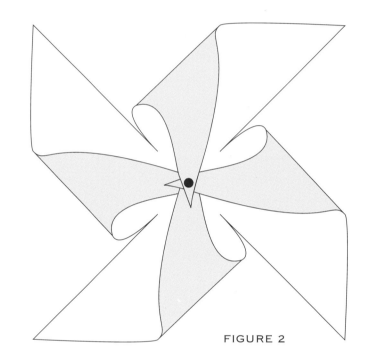

FIGURE 2

Christmas Lights

In 1882 Edward Johnson, a friend and cohort of Thomas Edison, invented electric Christmas tree lights: egg-sized globes of red, white, and blue. The bulbs were sold individually, each on a separate wire, and were prohibitively expensive for most people. After the turn of the century, economical strings of lights appeared.

Cones, Pods
& Grasses

❈ CORNHUSK CAROLERS ❈

In the fall, cornhusks are available in most craft shops and discount marts with craft departments. Despite the apparent sophistication of these singing angels, they are not difficult to make.

Materials

2 ounces (60 g) of cornhusks; heavy-, medium-, and fine-gauge floral wire; 3/4 inch diameter (2 cm) foam ball; dried cornsilk; white glue; glue gun; masking tape

1. Soak the cornhusks in a bucket of warm water for 15 to 30 minutes, until they're easy to bend and fold. (If you have trouble separating packaged cornhusks, just put the whole bundle in the bucket for a few minutes.)

2. Cut a 3-inch (8 cm) piece of heavy wire and make a fish hook in one end. Insert the other end into the foam ball.

3. Cut a piece of cornhusk about 2 inches (5 cm) wide and 5 inches (12 cm) long. Gather it in the middle. Place it on top of the ball and pull the wire until the hook is all the way into the foam, trapping the gathered husk in the center and fastening it to the ball. See Figure 1. Spread the husk over the ball to cover it; you now have the head. Twist a piece of fine-gauge wire around the neck. See Figure 2.

4. Now for the arms. Cut a 6-inch (15 cm) piece of medium-gauge wire and place it lengthwise along one side of a cornhusk that's about 7 inches (18 cm) long and 3 inches (4 cm) wide. Roll the husk snugly around the wire. Tie the center of this cylinder with fine-gauge wire. Trim the husk ends so the cylinder is

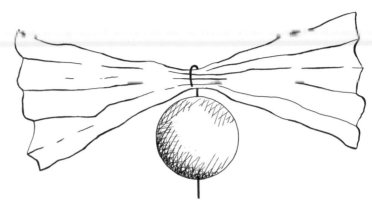

FIGURE 1

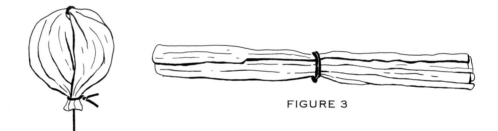

FIGURE 2

FIGURE 3

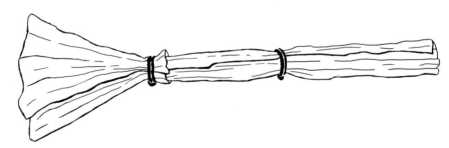

FIGURE 4

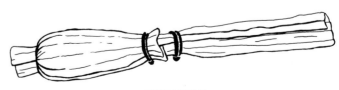

FIGURE 5

6 inches (15 cm) long. See Figure 3.

5. To make the sleeves, gather a 3-inch square of cornhusk around one arm about 1/2 inch (1 cm) from one end and tie it with fine wire. See Figure 4. Turn the husk inside out, back toward the center of the cylinder. Tie the sleeve at the center of the arm with fine wire. See Figure 5. Repeat on the other side to make the other sleeve.

6. Position the arms an appropriate distance below the head and wire them to the center "backbone" wire.

7. For the bodice, cut two pieces of husk 1-1/4 inches (3 cm) wide and about 3 inches long. To avoid unfinished edges, fold each long side to the center, so that each strip is 3/4 inch wide. Lay the center of each strip on a shoulder and bring the ends down the front and back, crossing at the waist in both front and back. Wrap a piece of fine wire around the waist and twist the wire ends together.

8. To make the skirt, first bend the arms up out of your way. Using your largest and best-looking husk first, place four to six large husks evenly around the chest and head, overlapping the waist by about 1/2 inch. See Figure 6. Wrap a piece of fine wire around the waist and fold the skirt down. Trim the bottom of the skirt to make it even.

9. Reposition the arms while they're still wet, arranging them so the angel will be ready to hold sheet music. Allow to dry completely, about four days.

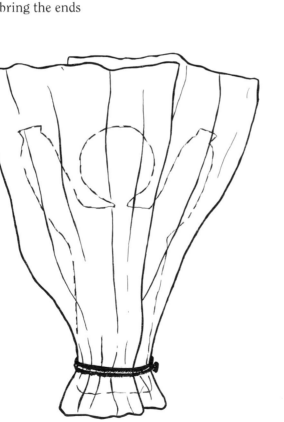

FIGURE 6

10. For angel hair, spread white glue on the head and wrap the cornsilk around the head. Glue down (or trim) any flyaway silks; no angel should have a bad hair day.

11. Glue two large husks together to make one thick one, using craft glue, and allow to dry. Cut out a pair of wings and some sheet music and hot-glue them to the usual places.

12. Cut a 2-inch piece of heavy-gauge wire and wrap it with masking tape. Bend it into a halo and insert it into the back of the head.

❋ PINECONE TREE ❋

An enormous cone from a sugar pine serves as a miniature Christmas tree.

Sugar Pines

Native to the mountains of the western United States, the sugar pine produces some of the largest cones in the world. They typically grow 12 to 15 inches long (30 to 40 cm), but they can exceed two feet (60 cm). A mature cone can weigh in at one full pound (500 g). Sugar pines are named for their unusual, sweet-tasting resin.

Materials

Pinecone about 12 inches (30 cm) tall; 6-inch (15 cm) vine wreath base; heavy-gauge floral wire; 4 feet (1.2 m) of miniature artificial pine garland; 4 feet of gold bead garland; metallic gold wired ribbon 1/16 inch (1.5 mm) wide; white spray paint; 25 to 30 pinecones 1/2 inch to 1 inch wide (1 to 3 cm); 3 large, red, artificial berries; miniature packages; 3 sprays of small, red, artificial berries

1. Fold a piece of heavy-gauge floral wire loosely in half and slip it around the cone between the two bottom rows of petals. Pull the wire tight against the center of the cone. Wire the cone twice more, positioning the wire ends in different places.
2. Using the wire ends, wire the cone to the vine base.

3. Spiral the pine garland and the gold bead garland down the length of the cone. To begin, wire them to the top of the cone; to end, hot-glue them to the wreath base.
4. Make 10 two-loop bows of the wired gold ribbon and wire them to the garland.
5. Spray the small pinecones white and allow them to dry. Hot-glue them randomly around the large cone.
6. Make a bow of beaded gold garland and one of wired gold ribbon, and glue or wire them to the top of the tree. Hot-glue the large red berries to the center of the bow.
7. Hot-glue the miniature packages around the base of the tree. Dress the packages up by hot-gluing small berries or cones to them. Hot-glue sprays of artificial berries between the packages.

❈ CONE CORSAGE ❈

In this ornament from nature, each component is attached to floral wire and then wired to the other items.

Materials

Cone or cone flower, 3 nutshell segments, floral wire, brown floral tape, narrow red ribbon

1. Wire a nutshell segment by holding it against a 5-inch (12 cm) piece of floral wire, toward the end of the wire, and wrapping brown floral tape around both shell and wire. The wrapped part of the shell will show, adding a two-tone design element, so make it a clean wrap. Continue to spiral the tape up the wire until the entire length is wrapped. Repeat for the remaining nutshells.

2. Wrap an 8-inch (20 cm) piece of floral wire with brown floral tape. Fold the wire loosely in half and slip it around the cone, between the two bottom rows of petals. Pull the wire tight against the center of the cone, and twist the wire ends together right next to the cone.

3. Make a six- or eight-loop bow from narrow red velvet ribbon and wire it around the center with a 4-inch (10 cm) piece of wire that you've wrapped with brown floral tape.

4. To assemble the ornament, first secure the three nutshell pieces in a V shape by taping around all three wires, taping their full lengths.

5. Position the cone at the top of the nutshells, with its wire pointing away from the nuts. Tape around its wire and the nutshell wires.

6. Shape the wrapped wires into a spiral-curving stem and cut any excess tape off the end of the stem.

7. Position the bow just behind the cone and twist its wires around the stem. Use the wire ends from the bow to attach the ornament to the tree.

✳ CARVED GOURDS ✳

To make a spectacular carved ornament, you need only a seasoned gourd (see "Gourds of the Season" on page 84), some leather dye, brown shoe polish, and a wood gouge. Look for U-shaped gouges (not the straight-edged or V-shaped ones) in a variety of small sizes wherever woodcarving tools are sold. The carved areas on a gourd are more porous than the uncarved shell and will dye a darker color.

Two-Color Gourd

Materials

Seasoned gourd, soft lead pencil, U-shaped gouge, brown leather dye, brown paste wax shoe polish, clean cloths, awl, decorative cord

1. Sketch your design on a piece of scratch paper; then pencil the design on the gourd.
2. Gouge out the appropriate areas, using different sizes of gouges as needed.

    To make clean cuts, first hold the gouge at a right angle to the gourd and make a stop cut. Then, holding the gouge at a low angle, shave a chip out of the surface, aiming toward the stop cut and stopping there (see Figure 1). Continue gouging out chips until the pattern is complete.

3. Rub brown leather dye over the entire gourd, using a clean rag. Wipe off the excess with a second rag. The dye will turn the carved areas a dark brown and the uncarved areas a medium to deep tan. Since each gourd takes the color differently, the shades of your ornaments will vary. Allow to dry.
4. Using a soft rag, rub paste wax shoe polish over the entire gourd to give it a natural-looking shine.
5. Using the awl, make a small hole through the stem for the hanger.
6. Thread the decorative cord through the hole and tie the ends in a bow.

———— ✳ ————

Long-Necked, Tri-Color Gourd

Materials

Same as for two-color gourd

1. Pencil the long, diagonal lines on the gourd.
2. Use a small gouge to carve out the lines you have drawn, creating an indentation along each one.
3. Decide which diamond shapes will be the darkest and gouge a series of chips from inside them. (Follow the above instructions for making clean cuts.)
4. With a clean rag, wipe brown leather dye over the carved triangles, then wipe if off with another rag. The dye will turn the porous gouged areas a dark brown and the uncarved areas a lighter color.
5. Rub brown paste wax shoe polish over the whole gourd and allow it to dry. Then gouge out the uncarved areas. The light-colored material underneath provides the pale third color.
6. Make a hanger as described above.

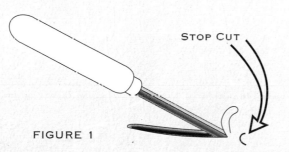

STOP CUT

FIGURE 1

⁕ Pine Needle Broom Ornament ⁕

Wherever pine trees grow, people have woven the fallen needles into baskets and other containers—yet another gift of the evergreen.

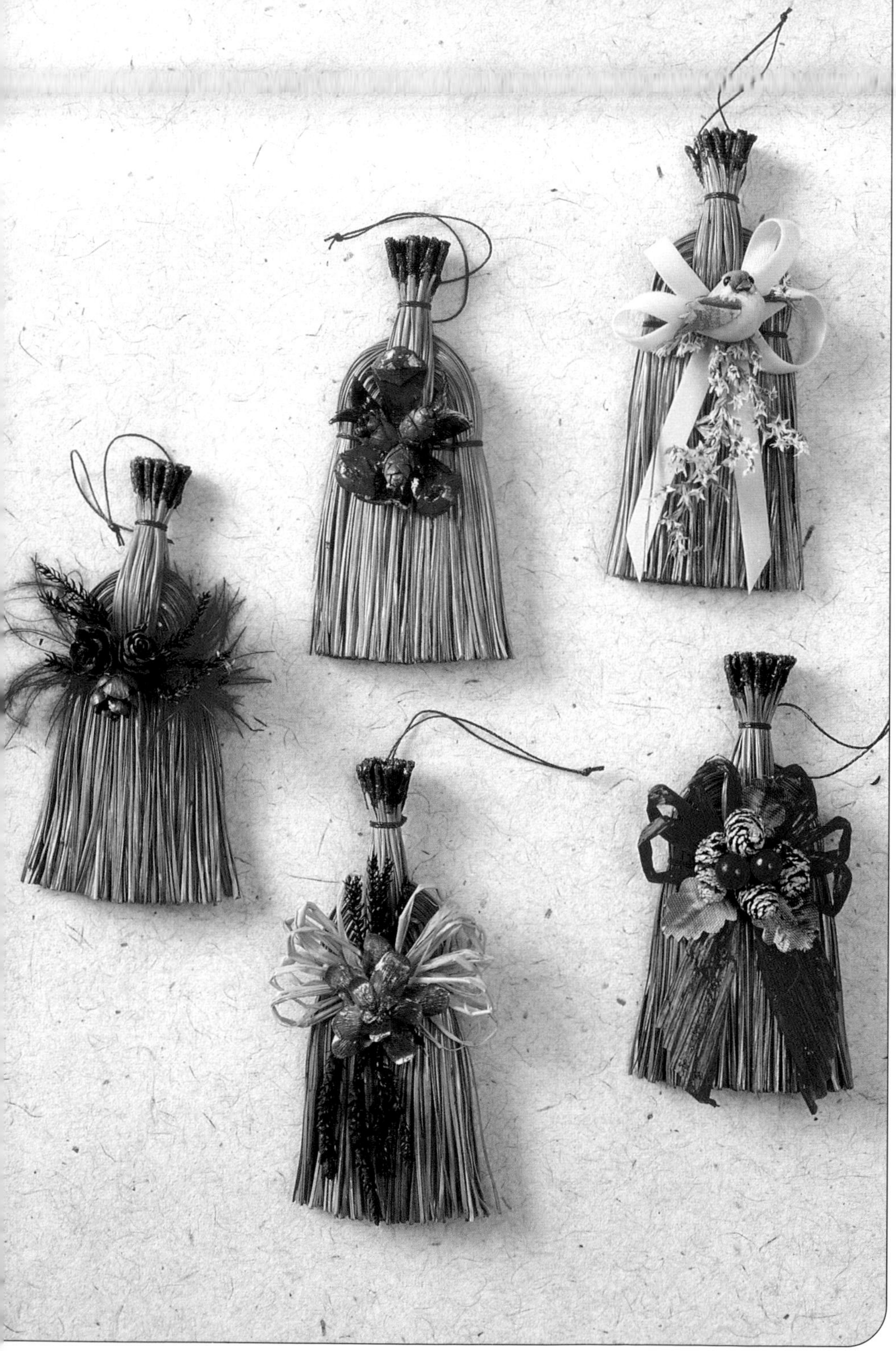

Materials

About 80 pine needle clusters, scissors, strong red thread, 4 twist ties, needle, acrylic spray, glue gun, various decorative materials

1. Soak the pine needles in hot water for 30 minutes, to make them pliable.
2. Make a bundle of 30 pine needle clusters, lining up the ends of the caps evenly.
3. Wrap a 12-inch (30 cm) piece of thread around the pine bundle just under the caps and tie a knot (see Figure 1). Knot the ends of the thread to form a hanger.

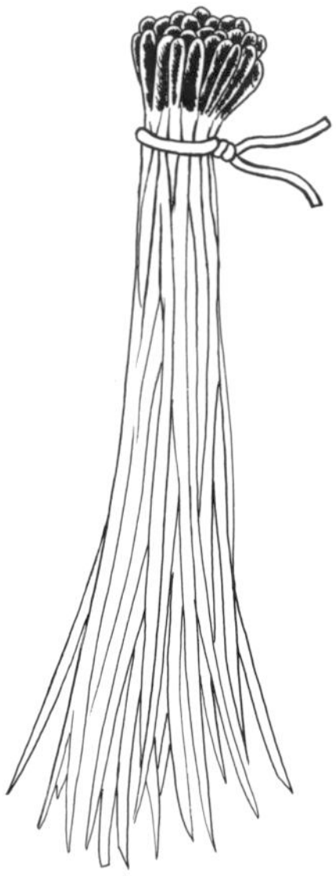

FIGURE 1

4. Make two bundles with 24 needle clusters each. Secure each bundle temporarily at both ends with the twist ties.
5. Separate the first bundle in half and insert the other two bundles into the opening, with the caps on one bundle to the right and the caps on the other bundle to the left. Push the two horizonal bundles up as far as possible.
6. Center a 30-inch (75 cm) piece of thread over the vertical bundle and wrap it twice around the

vertical bundle, right below the two horizontal bundles (see Figure 2). Knot the thread.

7. Thread the needle onto the right thread end. Bend the lower horizontal bundle down in an inverted U shape. Bring the needle around the right bundle and back through the middle bundle to secure (see Figure 3). Bring the needle around the left bundle and back through the center bundle.

8. Bend the top horizontal bundle down into an inverted U and sew it to the adjacent bundles in a similar fashion. Bring any loose threads to the front of the ornament and tie them off.

9. Cut the bottom of the broom off evenly and allow it to dry.

10. Spray the broom with clear acyclic.

11. Use the glue gun to attach small decorative materials. Shown, back row, left to right: red angel hair, hemlock cones, and greenery; pine petals and hemlock cone; white velvet bow, German statice, and tiny craft bird. Front row, left to right: dried greenery, raffia bow, hemlock cone flower; swiss straw bow, whitened cones, and red beads.

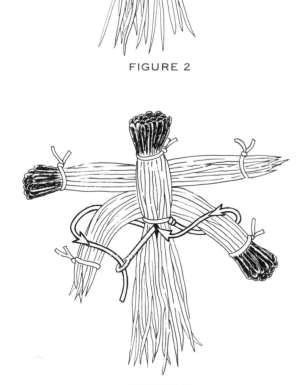

FIGURE 2

FIGURE 3

Pine Needles

Pine needles grow in bundles of two, three, or five. The bundles are held together and to the twig with a brown papery husk. Needles vary in length, from the 3/4-inch (2 cm) needles of the jack pine to the magnificent 18-inch (45 cm) needles of the longleaf pine so beloved by basket weavers. Each needle boasts a thick, waxy outer layer, or cuticle, that reduces the amount of moisture the tree loses and thus allows it to survive in areas that are too dry and cold for other species.

❈ BASKET TREE ❈

If you're an admirer of handmade baskets, why not turn your tree into a celebration of this fine craft? Miniature baskets abound. Wrap narrow red ribbon around the handles and finish with a bow at each end, or thread the ribbon through a large-eyed needle and weave the ribbon in and out of the basket itself.

And weave a few simple ornaments of your own: a woven square, a birdcage, a heart, and an Indian dream catcher. Reed (both round and flat) is available wherever basket-making supplies are sold, including most large craft stores.

Woven Square

Materials
12 inches (30 cm) of flat reed 5/8 inch (1.3 cm) wide, package of red fabric dye (optional), razor knife

1. If you want a two-color piece, cut the reed in half. Make up the fabric dye according to package instructions. Heat it to boiling, remove from the heat, and place half the reed in to soak. Remove it when it's slightly darker than you want. Rinse the dyed reed several times.
2. Soak the undyed reed in a pan of water for about 10 minutes. If the dyed reed has dried, soak it also, in a different pan.
3. Cut four pieces of reed about 2-1/2 inches (6 cm) long—two dyed and two undyed. Make your cuts at an angle.
4. Fold each piece in half and weave them together as shown in the photo, inserting the ends of each piece through the fold of another.

Birdcage

Materials
#0 round reed, small craft bird in nest, glue gun, narrow red ribbon

1. Soak all the reed in lukewarm water for 20 minutes.
2. Cut four 20-inch (50 cm) pieces of reed. These will be the ribs—the pieces that form the bottom and the sides of the birdcage. Place two ribs over the other two ribs at right angles, so they cross in the center.
3. The rest of the birdcage is *twined*, a simple but sophisticated-looking technique. Fold a 6-foot (1.8 m) piece of reed in half—this will be the *weaver*—and slip the folded middle around a horizontal group of ribs (see Figure 1). Bring both halves of the weaver around both ribs, so the two pieces of weaver cross on the other side of the ribs. Now take both pieces of the weaver around the other three pairs of ribs, crossing them over each other each time.

FIGURE 1

4. Go around the base a second time, twining around pairs of ribs (see Figure 2).
5. Now separate the pairs of ribs and twine loosely around the base one rib at a time (see Figure 3).

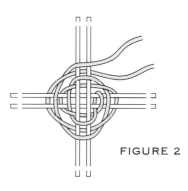

FIGURE 2

6. Continue to twine around the ribs, one at a time. As you work, shape the ribs upward to form the sides of the cage. Make sure the bottom is wide enough for the bird and nest.

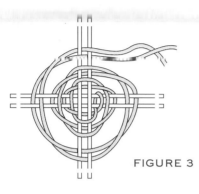

FIGURE 3

7. When you've twined two or three rows around the sides and the cage is taking shape, place the bird and nest in the center. Gather the ribs together at the top of the cage, and bring both ends of the weaver up to join them. Tie everything together with another piece of reed.

8. Tie a narrow red ribbon around the top of the cage.

———— ✳ ————

Heart

Materials
1 yard (90 cm) of 1/2-inch-wide (1.25 cm) paper-thin ash or thin, flexible reed, razor knife, white craft glue, alligator clips or mini clothespins, narrow red ribbon

1. Cut four pieces of ash 7-1/4 inches (18 cm) long. Cut each piece lengthwise into thirds. You should have 12 long, thin pieces. Discard two of them; you'll need a total of 10 for the heart.

2. Lay five pieces of ash vertically side by side.

3. Working toward one end of the group, weave a sixth piece horizontally over and under the first five (see Figure 1).

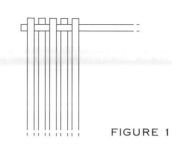

FIGURE 1

4. Weave another horizontal piece, alternating the vertical pieces it goes over and under. Weave the remaining pieces in similar fashion, making sure that no two adjacent weavers go over and under the same vertical piece (see Figure 2).

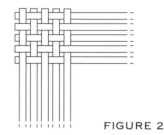

FIGURE 2

5. Tidy up the woven area to form a square, with the weavers parallel and the spaces between them about the same size.

6. Glue all intersections together. Place alligator clips at the edges to hold everything in place and allow to dry.

7. Turn the project with its point facing down toward you. Take the two outside strands, bring them toward the center, and cross the right one over the left (see Figure 3). Clip them together. Make sure you don't twist the weavers in the process; what was the top side on the glued section needs to be the top side in the clipped section.

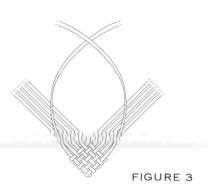

FIGURE 3

8. Take what are now the two outside strands and bring them toward the center. Bring the right one under the clipped end that points out to the right; weave the left one over and under the two ends (see Figure 4).

9. Again, take what are now the two outside weavers, and weave them over and under, making sure that they don't go over and under the same strands as their predecessors. Continue until all pieces of ash are woven.

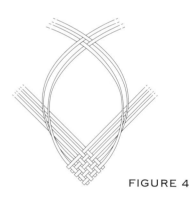

FIGURE 4

10. When all 10 ends are woven together—they should look like the first square you wove—tidy up the angles and glue all intersections together. Again, secure with clips until dry.

11. Fold the two ends of the piece together, point to point, and glue them together along the edges, from the points to about 1 inch (2.5 cm) up each side of the ornament. Clip and let dry.

12. Attach a bow and a hanger of red ribbon.

———— ✳ ————

Indian Dream Catcher

Materials

20 inches (50 cm) of #6 round reed or thin grapevine, 3-1/2 yards (3.3 m) of heavy, supple cord (leather thong or waxed linen, for example), feathers, beads

1. Make a 5-inch-diameter (12 cm) circle of round reed or vine. Tie the ends together with the cord or glue them together.

2. Tie a loop for hanging in one end of the cord. Then tie the cord onto the round base, about 3 inches (10 cm) from the hanging loop (see Figure 1).

3. The rest of the dream catcher is made with a series of loops. Move the cord about 2 inches (5 cm) to the right of where it's tied to the base and loop it around the base—that is, take the cord over the base, around behind it, and back to the front, bringing it, on that final step, through the loop it has formed (see Figure 1).

4. Make another loop 2 inches to the right, then another, and so on until the base is covered

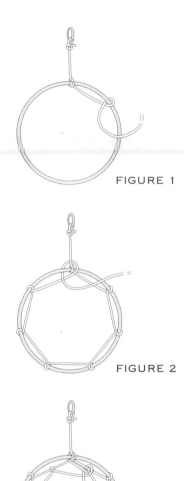

FIGURE 1

FIGURE 2

FIGURE 3

(see Figure 2).

Keep the cord taut as you work, but not so tight as to distort the circle. As you form each loop with your right hand, it's helpful to hold the previous loop with your left thumb and forefinger (the reverse if you're left-handed).

5. When you've been completely around the base, make the next loop in the center of the first straight string to your right. Continue around the circle in the same fashion, making a loop in the center of each straight piece of string (see Figure 3). Continue until the opening in the center is about 1 inch (2.5 cm) in diameter.

6. Many crafters finish at this point, knotting and cutting the string. Others continue with one final step. Loop around the innermost circle of string, placing the loops right next to each other and pulling each one tight. Cut the string close on the back of the project and fix it with a dot of glue.

7. For the hanging decoration, knot a piece of string at the bottom, thread onto it the beads of your choice, glue on a feather or two, and tie it to the bottom of the base.

Trimming the Tree

It's a yearly ritual: sawing off the bottom of the trunk until the Christmas tree stands level, only to discover that there's a huge gap in the foliage on one side. Sawing again, only to find a huge gap in the other side. Eventually you're down to a nub.

This is all less trying if the tree is a pine. Pine branches usually grow in whorls—more or less even layers—around the trunk, with one whorl added each year. Thus if you cut just below the branches on one side, you've probably cut just below the branches on all sides, leaving a decently symmetrical tree.

✳ SEED FLOWER ORNAMENTS ✳

Any attractive seeds can be used for these ornaments. Shown in the photo are pumpkin, cantaloupe, Japanese watermelon, striped sunflower, and Indian corn.

FIGURE 1

Materials

30 to 40 seeds, depending on size; 10 to 20 tiny seeds, such as rapeseed or white millet (common birdseed); 1-1/2-inch (4 cm) circle of thin cardboard or poster board, white craft glue; clear varnish spray; 5-inch (13 cm) length of heavy gold thread; 1-1/2-inch circle of felt

1. Lay a thin bead of glue around the edge of the cardboard circle.

2. Place the large seeds side by side around the circle, with about two-thirds of their length projecting out over the edge (see Figure 1). Allow the glue to dry.

3. Apply a circle of glue just below the seeds and add a second row of seeds, overlapping the first. Let dry. Apply a third row in the same way, overlapping the second.

4. Put a few drops of glue in the center of the ornament and add

the tiny seeds, filling the space. Let dry.

5. Spray the ornament with clear varnish and allow it to dry.

6. Squeeze a circle of glue around the back of the ornament. To make a hanger, fold the gold thread in half and place the ends on the back. Glue on the felt.

✳ GOURD SANTAS ✳

You can turn small gourds into Santas that wear the colors and expressions of your choice.

Gourds of the Season

While gourds are growing on their sprawling vines, they soak up lots of water and hold onto most of it. The same gourd that weighs 50 pounds (20 kg) fresh from the vine is feather-light after a few months of seasoning. As it dries, a gourd's skin hardens into a woody, waterproof shell that can be carved, painted, and dyed.

To season gourds, place them on a rack where air can circulate freely around them—either indoors or out. Turn them occasionally. Otherwise, ignore them completely. In three to six months, they'll turn off-white, beige, or brown, and their seeds will rattle when the gourd is shaken.

Materials

Seasoned gourd, soap, steel wool, soft lead pencil, acrylic paints, paint-brushes, black permanent marker, clear acrylic spray, awl or nail, long needle, embroidery floss

1. Soak the gourd in soapy water for half an hour, then scrub off all the dirt and mold with steel wool.
2. When the gourds are completely dry, sketch your design on the surface in pencil.
3. Paint the gourd with acrylic paints, beginning with the larger expanses, allowing each color to dry before adding another. Draw the features with the permanent marker.
4. When the paint is completely dry, spray the gourd with clear acrylic sealer.
5. Hold the Santa vertically and pencil dots on opposite sides of the stem. Using the awl or nail, punch a hole at each dot. Thread a long needle with embroidery floss and pass the needle through both holes. Knot the ends of the floss, forming a loop to serve as a hanger.

⁂ Ornaments for the Birds ⁂

In the dead of winter, birds need all the help they can get. These edible ornaments both decorate your yard and feed the birds, who will entertain you as they consume their Christmas dinner.

Materials
Large, attractive cone, peanut butter, wild birdseed, ribbon, floral wire

1. Turn the cone upside down and spread generous dollops of peanut butter on the petals. (For even better nutrition, combine equal parts of peanut butter and shortening with a little cornmeal.)
2. Press wild birdseed into the gooey mixture.
3. Make a decorative bow from your favorite ribbon and wire it to the top of the ornament, leaving enough excess wire to form a generous loop for hanging.

✿ CONES AND FEATHERS ✿

If you have a collection of small mementos—toby mugs, for example—you can wire them to a Christmas tree, where everyone can enjoy them. Fill in with bows of red paper ribbon, purchased ornaments, and a few creations of your own.

Upright Cones

Materials: large, attractive pinecone, spring-close clothespin, glue gun

1. Hot-glue the bottom of the cone to the top of one arm of the clothespin. Allow to dry.
2. Clip the clothespin, cone and all, to a tree branch. Rather than hanging from the branch, as wired cones do, this cone will sit upright on top of the branch.

——————— ✿ ———————

Feather Ornaments

Materials
White feather, gold spray paint, small spray of dried flowers, sweet gum ball, ribbon

1. Spray the feather lightly with gold paint and allow to dry.
2. Place the dried flowers and gum ball on the feather, with their stems pointing toward the quill end.
3. Tie the ribbon around the feather and both stems, holding the stems in place with the knot. Tie the ribbon in a bow.
4. Trim the stem ends of the flowers and gum ball.

——————— ✿ ———————

Sweet Gum Balls

Materials

Sweet gum balls, gold spray paint, floral wire

1. Spray the gum balls lightly with gold paint. Allow to dry.
2. Using floral wire, wire the gum balls to the ends of the tree branches.

Firs

Unlike pines, which have round needles and hanging cones, firs have flat needles attached to the twig in sprays, and cones that sit erect on top of the branches. One of the handsomest of all conifers is the balsam fir. Shaped like an illustrator's fantasy of a Christmas tree, it holds its soft, flat, fragrant needles extremely well after it's cut. (In the wild, individual needles remain on the tree for an unusually long three to five years.) For years woodsmen used the "Canada balsam" obtained from bark blisters as wound plasters, waterproof glue, and chewing gum.

Very similar is the Fraser fir, the preferred Christmas tree in much of the southern Unites States. Limited in range, it grows above 4,000 feet in the Appalachian Mountains.

The Douglas fir is native to the Pacific coasts of both Canada and the United States. When the western regions of those countries were being settled, the wood from Douglas firs supplied railroad ties, telegraph poles, and telephone poles that stretched for thousands of miles.

✶ GOURD BIRDHOUSES AND SEED GARLANDS ✶

What belongs in a tree? Birdhouses—or gourds decorated to look like birdhouses—and garlands of gourd seeds.

Gourd Birdhouse

Materials

Seasoned gourd, brown paste wax shoe polish, black acrylic paint, paintbrush, awl, super glue, gourd stem or wooden matchstick

1. Soak the gourd in soapy water for 30 minutes, then use steel wool to scrub off all the dirt and mold. Allow to dry.
2. Using a soft rag, rub brown paste wax shoe polish over the gourd and allow it to dry.
3. Paint a doorway in black acrylic paint.
4. With a narrow awl, make a small hole below the door and super-glue a length of gourd stem or wooden matchstick into the hole, to serve as a perch. Be careful not to let stray drops of glue fall on the gourd.

❋

Gourd Seed Garland

Materials

Gourd seeds, household bleach, red fabric dye, monofilament fishing line, large craft needle, ice pick (optional)

1. Clean all the flesh off the seeds and soak them for half an hour in a mixture of 1/2 cup (120 ml) household bleach to 1 quart (1 l) of water. Rinse the seeds in a colander.
2. Dye half the seeds red. In a two-quart (2 l) enamel or stainless steel pan, combine 2 cups (500 ml) water with 2 teaspoons powdered red fabric dye, and bring the mixture to a boil. Remove the dye from the heat and add the seeds. Let them sit for five to 10 minutes or until you like the color—keep in mind they'll be somewhat paler after they dry. Remove the seeds with a slotted spoon and spread them on newspaper to drain.
3. Reheat the dye and add the next batch of seeds, continuing the process until you've dyed as many seeds as want. If the dye weakens, add more powder.
4. Thread a piece of monofilament on the craft needle and knot the end. String the seeds while they're still wet, piercing them in the middle of a flat side. Alternate four red with four undyed seeds until the garland is the desired length. Knot the end of the thread and hang the garland to dry.

    Note: For easier stringing, pierce the seeds first with an ice pick.

❋ STRAW MARQUETRY ANGEL FACE ❋

An ancient art, straw marquetry involves using pieces of split straw as an applique. The most common is wheat straw—the long, hollow stalks that support the seed-bearing heads. If you live near a friendly wheat grower, ask to harvest a few handfuls, cutting it off near the ground. If not, wheat is available at many craft stores.

Materials

Wheat straw, craft knife, iron, sturdy paper (for example, a manila file folder), white craft glue, scissors

1. Cut off any attached seedheads and soak the straws in a mixture of three parts warm water to one part vinegar. (Vinegar helps to break down the starch in the straw.) How long the straw needs to soak can vary from 15 minutes to four hours, depending on the variety. If the supplier doesn't recommend a time, soak it until it's pliable. To test it, pinch the very end of the straw. If it springs back to your touch, it's ready.
2. With the craft knife, slit each straw down its full length and open it up. Iron the straw from the inside until it's flat and dry, being careful not to use an iron so hot that it scorches the straw. (Try permanent press.) Ironing will be easier if the straw doesn't rest on too soft a surface.
3. Transfer the patterns to sturdy paper and cut out the pieces. Be sure to cut *two complete wing sets*—two wing caps and two sets of feathers—and to flip one wing cap over when you add the straw splits, so your angel will have both right and left wings.

4. Apply glue to a pattern piece. Then cover it completely with straw splits, laying them side by side, shiny side up. All the straws on a pattern piece should be parallel. Make sure there aren't any gaps. Press the splits flat to the paper with your fingers or a burnishing tool.

5. After the glue is dry, turn the piece to the back and trim the straw ends with scissors, following the outline of the paper. To make the feathers look more featherlike, make 1/4-inch (6 mm) cuts around the edges (see the pattern).

6. Using the photo as a guide, glue the parts of the angel together. Start with the base as the bottom layer. Glue the feathers to the base one at a time, starting at the center and working outward on each side. Add the wing caps, then (in order) the face, hair, and halo.

(Pattern continued on next page.)

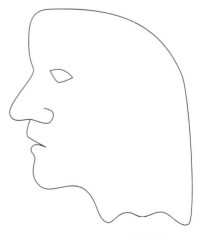

FACE

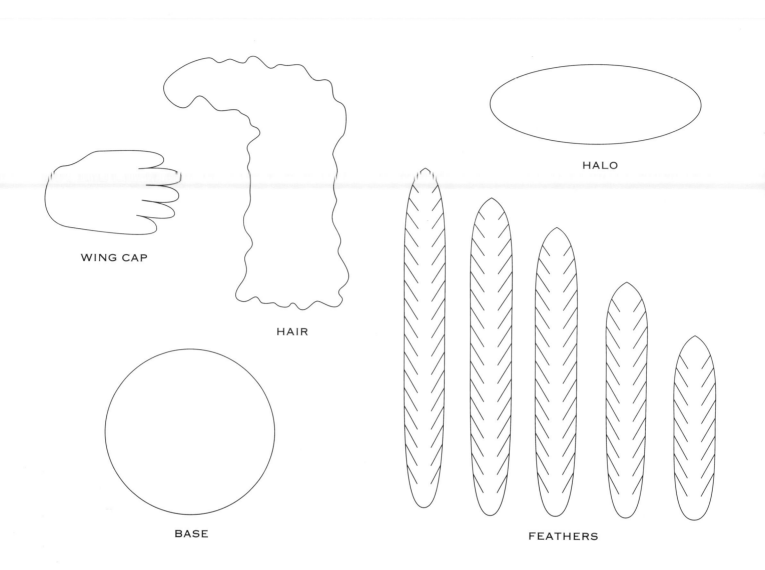

WING CAP

HAIR

HALO

BASE

FEATHERS

Spruces

Spruces are sharply conical evergreens with stiff, sharp, four-sided needles that grow singly all the way around the twigs. Their colors range from dark green to undeniably blue. (The ornaments on page 45 are shown on a blue spruce.) Spruces are a hardy bunch, growing north to the limit of trees, extending well into the sub-arctic tundra. Their soft, light wood is prized as sounding boards for pianos and for boat building. Although their needles drop rather quickly when dry, spruces are widely valued as Christmas trees. Some spruce lovers speculate that the tree's natty appearance explains the complimentary "all spruced up."

⁂ Australian Pine Cone Wreath ⁂

Huge trees with long, graceful needles, Australian pines produce tiny cones.

Materials

9-inch (22 cm) piece and 18-inch (45 cm) piece of heavy-gauge floral wire, brown floral tape, drill with 1/16-inch (1.5 mm) bit, 15 Australian pine cones, cotton pod, narrow red ribbon, clear acrylic spray

1. Wrap both pieces of wire with floral tape.
2. Drill a hole crosswise through each cone.
3. String the cones on the 18-inch piece of wire.
4. Bend the wire into a circle about 3 inches (7 cm) in diameter and twist the ends around each other, then into a small loop.
5. Wrap the 9-inch piece of wire around the cotton pod and attach it to the wreath, opposite the loop.
6. Spray the wreath lightly with clear acrylic sealer.
7. Attach a hanger of narrow red ribbon.

✻ WHEAT ORNAMENTS ✻

The rich beige tones of wheat look stunning against a dark evergreen.

Materials
Floral wire, wheat, ribbon, decorative pod and glue gun (optional)

1. Wire the stalks of wheat together just below the seedheads.
2. Make a full bow and wire it together around the center, leaving long wire ends. Wire the bow to the wheat.
3. If you like, you can hot-glue a decorative pod to the center of the bow.
4. Use the wire ends to attach the ornament to the tree.

Wheat Tree Topper

Wire the long stalks of wheat vertically to the center of the tree—either on the back of the tree, so the fanned wheat bursts star-like from the top of the tree, or to the front, so that the long stalks are visible.

Materials

About 60 stalks of wheat 18 to 20 inches (45 to 50 cm) long, floral wire, glue gun, short stalks of wheat, ribbon, German statice, paper or cornhusk flower (optional)

1. Soak the wheat in warm water for about 1 hour, or until it's flexible enough to bend.
2. Lay the stalks of wheat together in a bundle with their tops even, and wire them together about 3 inches (7 cm) below the bottom of the seedheads. Spread the seedheads out in a fan shape.
3. Hot-glue short stalks of wheat to the back of the fan as necessary to make a full ornament, with their stalks in the center and their seeds fanning out.
4. Make a large, multi-loop bow and wire it on top of the other wire.
5. Hot-glue sprigs of German statice into the bow; the bow should look well filled, and you should use a lot of statice.
6. If desired, hot-glue a paper or cornhusk flower in the center of the bow.

Edible Evergreens

Conifers are fine food sources for wildlife. Once a cone releases the seeds it's been protecting, the feast is on. (Hence the need, from the tree's point of view, for protection.) Bears, coyotes, rabbits, squirrels, chipmunks, grouse, pheasants, and quail eat the fat- and protein-rich seeds of the local species, and humans nibble on the nuts from pinyon pines. Deer, moose, squirrels, and rabbits browse on the branches, and porcupines gnaw on the bark.

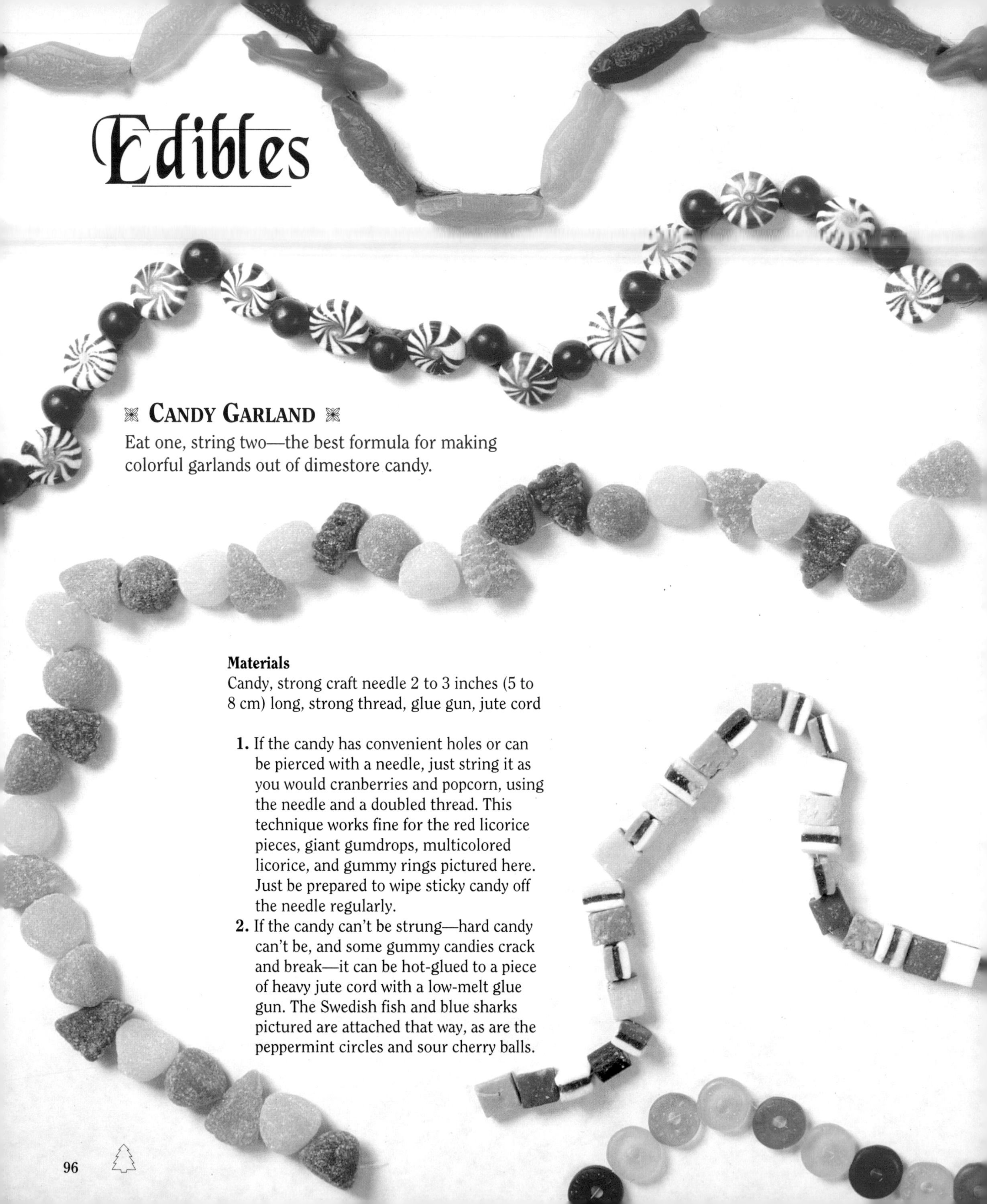

Edibles

✤ CANDY GARLAND ✤

Eat one, string two—the best formula for making colorful garlands out of dimestore candy.

Materials

Candy, strong craft needle 2 to 3 inches (5 to 8 cm) long, strong thread, glue gun, jute cord

1. If the candy has convenient holes or can be pierced with a needle, just string it as you would cranberries and popcorn, using the needle and a doubled thread. This technique works fine for the red licorice pieces, giant gumdrops, multicolored licorice, and gummy rings pictured here. Just be prepared to wipe sticky candy off the needle regularly.

2. If the candy can't be strung—hard candy can't be, and some gummy candies crack and break—it can be hot-glued to a piece of heavy jute cord with a low-melt glue gun. The Swedish fish and blue sharks pictured are attached that way, as are the peppermint circles and sour cherry balls.

✱ FRONTIER CHRISTMAS ✱

Combine a rustic log cabin...some prickly wreaths made from sycamore pods...old-fashioned popcorn balls and gingerbread...a tree topper of rough-woven burlap—and you have the makings of a tree that celebrates the do-it-yourself, make-your-own-fun frontier spirit. Fill in with simple bows of paper ribbon, tied or wired to the branches, and sprigs of German statice placed randomly around the tree. For the gingerbread figures, see the recipe on page 65.

Log Cabin

Materials

8-1/2- by 11-inch (21 X 27 cm) manila folder or other lightweight cardboard, scissors, craft cement or white glue, light brown spray color, straight pretzels about 2-1/2 inches (6 cm) long, oyster crackers, awl or large nail, craft pick or toothpick, heavy string, bite-size frosted shredded wheat cereal, black acrylic paint, small flat paintbrushes, acrylic spray

1. Enlarge the pattern or use it as a guide to draw your own. Each wall should be no more than 2-1/2 inches wide (so the pretzels will fit). Height is optional. Cut the cabin out of the manila folder. Fold on the fold lines, overlap the walls and tabs, and glue the cabin together. Allow to dry.
2. Cut a rectangle about 3-1/2 by 5 inches (9 X 13 cm) from the manila folder for the roof.
3. Lightly spray cabin (inside and out) and one side of the roof with light brown spray—for example, floral sandalwood color.
4. Glue the pretzels to the walls, beginning at the bottom and cutting them to fit (see Figure 1).
5. Glue one or two pretzels vertically at each corner, to fill the space and cover the cardboard.
6. Matching the short edges, fold the roof in half. Rest the roof on the cabin's roof line tabs, and glue it to the cabin. Allow to dry.

Photocopy pattern at 285%.

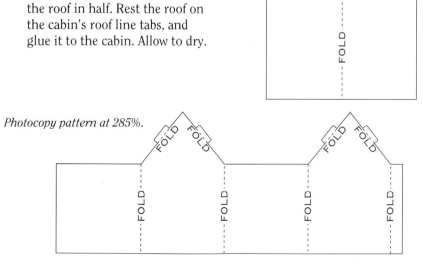

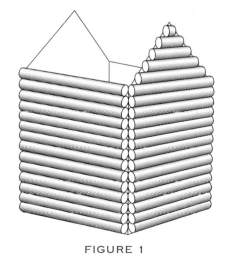

FIGURE 1

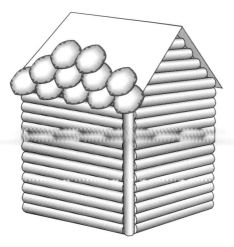

FIGURE 2

7. Using the awl or nail, punch a small hole in the center of the roof. Tie an 18-inch (45 cm) piece of string to the center of the floral pick, and thread the other end of the string through the hole, inside to outside. This will serve as the ornament's hanger. The floral pick should fit into the long fold of the roof and provide extra support.

8. To shingle the roof, glue a row of oyster crackers along the bottom of each side of the roof. Allow that row to dry, then add another row, staggering and overlapping the second row. Allow to dry, then repeat until the roof is covered (see Figure 2).

9. To make the chimney, glue two pieces of shredded wheat to the roof.

10. Paint the windows and door, using black acrylic paint.

11. Apply two coats of acrylic spray, allowing time to dry between coats.

Sycamore Wreaths

Materials
Glue gun, sycamore balls or sweet gum balls, German statice, nandina berries or other firm, red berries

1. Hot-glue the sycamore balls to each other to form a circle. Allow the glue to dry.
2. Hot-glue sprigs of German statice and nandina berries evenly around the wreaths.

Popcorn Balls

Makes 6-8 balls

1/4 cup (25 g) margarine or butter
1/2 cup (120 ml) light corn syrup
1/2 cup sugar
1/2 teaspoon salt
8 cups (2 l) popped corn
Yellow cellophane
Heavy string

1. In a very large (about 4-quart, or 4-l) pot, heat margarine, corn syrup, sugar, and salt over medium-high heat, stirring constantly until sugar is dissolved.
2. Add popped corn and cook, stirring constantly, until all the popcorn is coated, about 3 minutes. Allow to cool just until comfortable to touch (don't let it harden).
3. Wet your hands, and shape the popcorn into balls about 3 inches (8 cm) in diameter. Place balls on waxed paper and allow to cool completely.
4. Wrap each ball in yellow cellophane, twist closed, and tie with string, leaving a long enough tail to tie to the tree.

Moon and Star Tree Topper

2 pieces of brown burlap about 14 inches (35 cm) square (for the moon), 2 pieces of white burlap about 6 inches (15 cm) square (for each star), fiberfill, glue gun, fabric paint or marker, monofilament fishing line, 12-inch (35 cm) piece of medium-gauge wire

1. Using the pattern below as a guide, draw a moon about 12 inches (30 cm) tall. Cut out the pattern.
2. Lay the two large squares of burlap on top of each other. Pin the pattern to the pieces of burlap, and cut out two moons.
3. Hot-glue them together around the edges, about 1/2 inch (1 cm) in from the edge, leaving an opening about 2 inches (5 cm) long. Allow the glue to dry.
4. Stuff the moon with the fiberfill, then glue the opening closed.
5. Use fabric paint or marker to shade cheeks. If necessary, trim any rough edges of fabric.
6. Make the star by the same method.
7. With the monofilament, hang the star from the moon.
8. On the back side of the moon, thread the wire into and back out of the burlap, and wire the ornament to the tree.

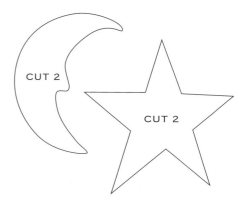

CUT 2

CUT 2

❋ FRUIT TABLE TREE ❋

Want to make the kids happy? Take the apples and oranges back
out of their stockings, put the fruit on a Christmas tree, and put
a lot of too-sweet, nutrition-free candy in the stockings.

Materials
Artificial tree about 25 inches (63
cm) tall, 16-inch-square (40 cm)
cloth napkin, heavy string, sprigs of
dried mountain mint (or other large,
firm-leaved herb), dried apple slices,
preserved orange slices, 10 dried
pomegranates

1. Gather the napkin around the
   base of the tree and tie it around
   the trunk with string. Fold the
   edges of the napkin over to hide
   the string.
2. Hot-glue sprigs of mint to as
   many branch ends as possible.

3. Hot-glue the apple and orange
   slices to the tips of tree branches,
   positioning them randomly
   around the tree.
4. Hot-glue the pomegranates to the
   tree. Since they're heavier than
   the other fruit, position them
   closer to the tree trunk.

❋ ORANGE-FILLED ORNAMENTS ❋

The scent of citrus is as much a part of Christmas as the fragrance
of evergreens.

Materials
3-inch-diameter (8 cm) plastic pot
pourri ornament, 1/4 cup (60 ml)
dried orange granules, glue gun,
2 preserved orange slices, 2 1-inch
(2.5 cm) cinnamon sticks, 2 bay
leaves, whole star anise, raffia

1. Place the orange granules in the
   ornament and close it securely.
2. Using the photo as a guide, hot-
   glue the bay leaves in place.
3. Hot-glue a whole orange slice
   over the junction of the bay
   leaves. Cut the remaining orange
   slice in half and glue the halves
   on either side of the whole slice,
   tucking the straight edges under
   slightly.
4. Hot-glue the cinnamon sticks
   over the bay leaves and under the
   half slices.
5. Hot-glue the star anise in the
   center of the whole orange slice.
6. Make a raffia loop for a hanger
   and tie it to the ornament's plastic loop. Make a raffia bow and tie
   it to the bottom of the hanger.

❈ PASTA E FAGIOLI ❈

One of the best-loved winter soups in the world, *pasta e fagioli* ("pasta fah-ZOOL," sort of) is a gift from the good cooks of Italy. The pasta-and-bean soup is so warming and comforting on a raw December night that a Christmas tree in its honor is not too extravagant a gesture.

Pasta Ornaments

Materials
Dried pasta, glue, ribbon or decorative cord

1. Arrange the pasta into interesting patterns and glue it together, using the glue of your choice. Tacky glue works well, and it dries clear and virtually invisible, even though you need a substantial bead to hold two pieces together. Hot-glue is easy to apply and holds the pieces very securely, but it tends to show if you're not careful.
2. Glue a ribbon hanger to the back of the ornament or tie it to a handy portion.

———— ❈ ————

Bean Balls

Materials
Satin balls, dried beans, glue gun, glitter glue sticks, clear acrylic spray, decorative cord

1. Beans are fairly heavy, so the smaller balls are better than the large ones. Working from the top down, apply hot glitter glue to a section of the ball and press the beans one at a time into the glue. Use various types and colors of beans to make designs.
2. Spray the finished ornament with clear acrylic.
3. Hot-glue a loop of decorative cord to the top as a hanger.

⌘ OKRA ⌘

An African native, okra has been introduced to the other parts of the world by African immigrants who carried the seeds and the cooking methods with them. Okra is good fried, stewed, or painted.

Materials
Whole okra pods, acrylic paints, paintbrush, glitter (optional), clear varnish spray, embroidery floss, glue gun

1. Place the okra in a warm, moisture-free place to dry for about two months.
2. Paint the pods. If desired, dust a few of them with fine glitter while the paint is still wet.
3. When the okra are completely dry, spray them with clear varnish.
4. Hot-glue a loop of embroidery floss to each stem to form a hanger.

❈ CINNAMON SANTAS ❈

The scent of cinnamon is a pleasant addition to a Christmas tree.

Materials

Cinnamon stick about 6 inches (15 cm) long, 2 cinnamon sticks 2-1/2 to 3 inches (6 to 8 cm) long, glue gun, acrylic paints, tiny cotton ball, red ribbon 1/16 inch (1.5 mm) wide for hanger

1. On the bottom of the two short cinnamon sticks   the "arms"— paint red and white cuffs.
2. Paint a Santa face and a red hat on the long cinnamon stick.
3. Hot-glue the cinnamon sticks together, with the long one in the center.
4. Make a loop of the red ribbon and glue it to the top of the "head." Glue a cotton ball to the hat.

Pet Safety

Pets will eat anything, including things that will harm them. Metal ornament hooks can stick in their throats, and long pieces of string, yarn, tinsel, or cellophane can get stuck in the twists and turns of their intestines. The first canine who pigged out on chocolate is probably responsible for the phrase "sick as a dog."

If you have a curious and chronically hungry pet (two redundancies right there), you might forgo any food-based ornaments. Even if the food itself isn't harmful, your pet may get into other trouble while it's foraging.

❊ STRAWBERRY CORN ❊

With its rich, red color and endearing size, strawberry corn is a fine ornamental for Christmas crafting. Widely available as seed corn for the home garden or as full grown ears in the fall, strawberry corn normally grows a mere 2 to 3 inches (5 to 8 cm) long.

White Ornament

Materials: ear of strawberry corn, gold spray paint, decorative gold cord, glue gun, dusty miller leaves, white annual statice, pink straw-flowers, white globe amaranth

1. Remove any husks, spray the corn lightly with gold paint, and allow it to dry.
2. Hot-glue a loop of gold cord to the top, to serve as a hanger.
3. Hot-glue the leaves and flowers to the top and bottom of the orna-ment in the order listed, using the photo as a guide.

Scotch Plaid Ornament

Materials

Acrylic spray, glue gun, thin red rib-bon, seedheads from wild grasses, plaid ribbon, red and pink globe ama-ranth

1. Coat the cob with acrylic spray and allow it to dry.
2. Hot-glue a loop of thin red ribbon to the top.
3. Hot-glue the seedheads around the top.
4. Cut a piece of plaid ribbon long enough to circle around the top and hot-glue it to the corn.
5. Finally, hot-glue the globe amaranths in the center.

Scotch Pine

One of only three conifers native to Britain, the Scotch pine has 2- to 3-inch (5 to 8 cm) needles in bundles of two. It has been exported extensively to the United States for Christmas tree farms and reforestation.

❋ DECOUPAGE EGGS ❋

Decoupage eggs are literally a cut-and-paste project, very simple to do. They are, of course, as fragile as eggshells.

Materials

White eggs, fork or straight pin, white glue, decorative paper, small paintbrush, clear acrylic spray, 9-inch (23 cm) piece of fine-gauge wire; small beads, spangles, or tassels; wire clippers or heavy shears

1. To empty out the egg, wash and dry it, then make a small hole in the narrow end, using a fork tine or a straight pin. Make a slightly larger hole in the wide end (now the bottom). Working over a bowl, blow on the top hole, forcing the white and yolk out of the bottom. Rinse the eggshell again and set it aside to dry.

2. Cut out small pieces of decorative papers—giftwrap, pictures from magazines, note cards, whatever is handy. Glue the pieces of paper to the egg.

3. When the glue is dry, coat the entire egg with clear acrylic spray. Apply a second and third coat of acrylic, allowing the eggs to dry after each application.

4. Insert the fine wire through the top and bottom holes in the egg. Add flat spangles, small beads, or a jingle bell at top and bottom.

5. At the top of the egg, twist the excess wire into a loop, twist the loop closed, and cut off the excess wire. Tie a piece of decorative cord or string to the wire loop to serve as a hanger.

6. At the bottom of the egg, wrap the wire end around the bottom bead or tassel and trim off the excess wire.

Paint, Glitter & Glue

❋ PYRAMIDS ❋

These contemporary-looking, three-dimensional pyramids are easy to make.

Materials

Heavy mat board, razor knife, glue gun, acrylic paints, paintbrush, paint pens, glitter glue, craft gems, bead cap, bead, heavy thread, threads in various colors, colored tree icicles, needle

1. Using paper, pencil, and a ruler or straightedge, draw an isosceles triangle 4-1/2 inches (11 cm) on its long sides and 3 inches (7.5 cm) on its short side.
2. Trace the triangle three times onto heavy mat board and cut out the three triangles with a razor knife.
3. Using a clear glue stick, hot-glue the three triangles together along their long edges to create a pyramid, leaving the bottom open.

4. Paint the pyramid with acrylic paints, using whatever patterns of lines and squiggles appeal to you.

5. Lay a long bead of glitter glue along the edges where the three triangles meet. Add dots of glitter glue on the three surfaces. Add a sizeable "puddle" of glitter glue and place a craft gem in the center.

6. Glue the bead cap on top of the pyramid.

7. To make a tassel, form a 1-inch-thick (2.5 cm) bundle of 14-inch (35 cm) lengths of colored thread, plus a few colored Christmas tree icicles. Fold the bundle in half and wrap a piece of heavy thread around it about 1 inch from the fold. Knot the thread, leaving two very long tail ends.

8. Thread both long ends through the needle, so that you're working with a doubled thread, and bring the needle up through the top of the pyramid. Thread the bead onto the needle, push it down to the top of the pyramid, and knot the thread right above the bead, to hold it in place. Tie the ends of the thread in a loop to form a hanger.

❊ MINI WREATHS ❊

Combine a few miniature wreath bases, a little glitter glue, some odds and ends, and a sense of fun, and you can whip up delightfully outrageous ornaments in no time.

Materials

4- or 5-inch (10 to 13 cm) vine wreath base, glue gun, glitter glue sticks, shiny cord, trinkets

1. Just wrap the wreaths with something long, thin, and shiny, hot-gluing the ends in place.
2. Hot-glue the trinkets of your choice to the wreath.
3. Examine the photo for examples to either embrace or avoid. Back row, left to right: 1) Gold tinsel mini garland plus red, gold, and silver plastic beads. 2) White buttons, white mini garland, and dollops of red glitter glue. 3) Plastic tube beads strung on floral wire and gold tinsel mini garland. 4) Multistrand telephone wire, gold mini garland, and gold jingle bells.
Front row, left to right: 1) Beads strung on floral wire and gold mini garland. 2) Purple metallic cord and lavender buttons. 3) Plastic beads, dollops of red glitter glue, and gold mini garland.

Two-Tone Firs

Many firs have needles with different colors on top and bottom. The Fraser fir is rich green above and blue below. The silver fir is dark green on top and silver underneath.

✳ MARBLED ORNAMENTS ✳

These memorable ornaments started out as inexpensive satin balls. They got their color from marbling, a craft that is becoming increasingly popular. To make them, you'll need the acrylic fabric paints available at any craft store, plus two items that are available only where marbling supplies are sold. One is aluminum sulfate, a white powder that acts as a mordant—that is, it makes paint bond with fabric. The other is methyl cellulose, a form of wood pulp, which is used to thicken water.

Materials

White satin balls, aluminum sulfate, clothesline and clothespins, methyl cellulose, household ammonia, 2 buckets or deep bowls, acrylic fabric paints, eye dropper, knitting needle or chopstick (or any object with a single long point)

1. Stir 1/2 cup (118 ml) aluminum sulfate into 1 gallon (4 l) of hot water until the powder is dissolved. Immerse each ball for 10 to 15 seconds, remove it from the mordant, and hang it to dry, using the clothespins to attach it to the clothesline.

2. Stir 4 tablespoons of methyl cellulose into 1 gallon of warm water. When the methyl cel has dissolved, stir in 2 tablespoons of ammonia. Pour this "bath" into a deep bowl or bucket and allow it to sit for about 12 hours. When you're ready to marble, pour clean water in the other bucket.

3. If there are loose threads on any of the balls, unwrap the stray end until you have a good "tail" of thread, tie it around the ball's hanger, and trim the end.

4. Pour each color of fabric paint into a small container and add clean water a little at a time until the paints are about the consistency of whole milk. Drop just a drop on the bath. If the paint sinks, add more water.

5. Skim the bath by drawing a strip of newspaper over it.

6. With the eye dropper, drop individual drops of paint onto the bath; they should float on the surface. Add drops of other colors until the surface is covered.

7. Holding the knitting needle vertically over the bath, insert the tip into the bath and move it back and forth, creating swirling patterns in the paint.

8. Holding a ball by its hanger ring, dip it straight down into the bath, immersing it completely. Then bring it straight up out of the bath.

9. Rinse the ball by dipping it in the bucket of clean water, then bringing it back out.

10. Hang the ball on the clothesline to dry. Skim the surface of the bath, add new drops of paint, and marble another ball. Continue in this fashion until you have as many as you want.

11. Check the hangers on the balls. If any are loose, pull them up to give yourself some working room and cement them to the balls with white craft glue.

⁂ GLITTER GLUE BALLS ⁂

Go for baroque! To create insanely ornate ornaments, latch onto glitter glue sticks of many colors.

Materials
White satin Christmas balls, glue gun, glitter glue

1. Apply glitter glue directly to the Christmas balls, changing colors as you go along. Dots, vertical lines, wavy lines—live it up.

2. Work the top of the ball and let it cool, then work the bottom and let it cool, going back and forth until the ornament is overdone by any standard of sober good taste.

❋ GLITTER GLUE SNOWFLAKES ❋

For this project you'll need one of the transparent glue pads available where glue guns and glue sticks are sold. The advantage of the pads is that hot glue won't stick to them.

Materials

Pencil, paper, glue pad, glue gun, glitter glue, decorative cord

1. Draw a basic snowflake design, using pencil and paper.
2. Place the drawing under the glue pad. Then draw your snowflakes in hot glue, following the lines of the original design.
3. Allow the snowflake to cool, then lift it off the pad.
4. Add a hanger of decorative cord.
5. If your tree is already full, you can press the snowflakes onto your windowpanes, where they will adhere nicely and serve as window decorations.

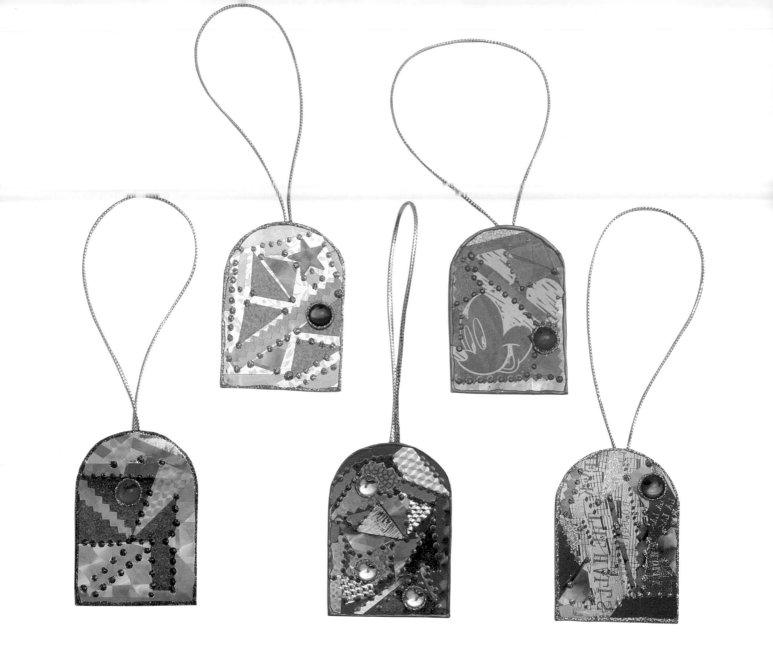

❋ MAGNETIC ORNAMENTS ❋

Discount marts sell sheets of material that are magnetic on one side and sticky on the other—which means you can cut out the shapes of your choice, remove the protective sheet from the sticky side, and press on bits of decorative paper. After Christmas is over, pull off the hangers and stick the magnets on the refrigerator.

Materials
Sheets of magnetic material, bits of old Christmas cards, glittery paper, craft jewels, glue gun, glitter glue sticks, decorative cord

1. Cut the magnetic sheets into the shapes of your choice.
2. Peel off the protective paper from the sticky side of the magnet and press the bits of paper into it, creating a design as you go.
3. Decorate the ornaments with dots and lines of glitter glue; make some of the dots large enough to hold a craft jewel. Encircle the entire ornament with a bead of glitter glue.
4. Fold the decorative cord loosely in half and glitter-glue it to the back of the ornament.

✳ SPANGLE BALLS ✳

These brilliant ornaments will reflect every light on your tree.

Materials

Satin tree balls; shiny, round, flat spangles 3/4 inch (2 cm) in diameter; glue gun; clear and glitter glue sticks; narrow ribbon

1. Beginning at the bottom of the ball, hot-glue rows of spangles around it, using clear glue sticks and overlapping the spangles from side to side and from top to bottom.

2. When the ball is covered, encircle the metal ring at the top of the ball with five or six dots of glitter glue.

3. If desired, you can dot glitter glue on each spangle. The green ball in the center, for example, boasts dollops of red glitter glue on each green spangle.

4. Tie a piece of narrow ribbon to the ball's built-in loop to serve as a hanger.

❋ Gold and Silver Tree ❋

Some of the best-looking trees rely on quantity as well as quality. A riot of ornaments—with no branch left untouched—is delightful to look at...and look at...and look at. To achieve this effect, combine the purchased ornaments you're especially fond of with your own handcrafted decorations.

Patterned Gold Ball

Materials

Purchased glass ball, glitter, extra-hold hairspray in pump bottle, bristle or sponge brush with fine tip

1. Sketch several designs with pencil and scratch paper until you find one you like.
2. Pour some of the hairspray into a small bowl.
3. Dip the brush into the hairspray and paint a portion of the design onto the ball.
4. While the sticky spray is still wet, sprinkle it heavily with glitter.
5. Continue in this fashion until the design is complete. While the balls shown have matching glitter, contrasting colors can be very effective.

Feather Ornament

Materials
Small white feather, lace ribbon

1. Tie the ribbon around the quill end of the feather.
2. Position the feather on a tree branch.

Miniature Package

Materials
Small box, patterned foil giftwrap, white craft glue, blue ribbon, white beads

1. Wrap the package with the giftwrap.
2. Glue the ribbon around the package in a cross shape.
3. Glue the white beads to the intersection of the ribbon.

Metallic Thread Ornament

Materials
Small piece of styrofoam in desired shape, metallic silver thread, white glue, narrow blue ribbon

1. Wrap the metallic thread around the foam base, securing the end under the first few wraps. As much as possible, wrap in the same direction, so that the threads are parallel on each section of the ornament.
2. When the foam is completely covered, secure the tail end of the thread with a tiny dab of glue on the center top of the ornament.
3. Tie the ornament with the blue ribbon, dividing it into four vertical segments. Finish with a bow, hiding any trace of the glue.
4. Add a loop of metallic thread, tying it underneath the blue ribbon.

✳ PAINTED GLASS ORNAMENTS ✳

Frosted glass ornaments are excellent for painting. On clear ornaments, the painted design shows through to the other side and distorts both sides. The balls above are decorated in designs reminiscent of the American Southwest.

Materials
Frosted glass balls, soft lead pencil, acrylic paints, narrow-tipped paint brush, narrow ribbon

1. Sketch your design on the ball in soft-lead pencil.
2. Paint the design in the colors of your choice.
3. Attach a hanger of narrow ribbon.

✻ SHELL TREE ✻

This elegant, gold-and-white tree displays a fine collection of seashells. Gold bows act as fillers.

Materials
Seashells, glue gun or drill with 1/16-inch (1.5 mm) bit, gold decorative cord, gold ribbon 1 inch (2.5 cm) wide, floral wire

1. Attach the shells to loops of decorative cord. If the shell has an opening, just thread the cord through the hole and tie it in a loop.
2. If not, you can drill one. The results are tidy, but you risk breaking some shells. The other option is to hot-glue the cord to the shell, using as little glue as possible and positioning it inconspicuously.

❋ BEACH SANTAS ❋

If you pick up small pieces of flotsam as you stroll along the beach, only to toss them in a drawer until you eventually throw them away, you now have something to do with them. Both shells and small pieces of driftwood make good Santas. Even grungy shells clean up well when they're bleached.

Clamshell Santas

Materials
Clamshells, household bleach, acrylic paints, paintbrushes, fine-tipped permanent markers, liquid "snow," glue gun

1. Wash the shells, scrape off any remaining debris, and soak them for two or three days in a mixture of one part bleach to three parts water. Allow to dry.

2. Paint Santa faces on the shells, giving them the personality of your choice. Use the permanent markers to draw the facial features. Add a textured band of "fur" on the cap, using one of the liquid-snow products that become three-dimensional when they dry.

3. Knot the ends of the ribbon to form a loop, and hot-glue it to the back of the shell.

────── ❋ ──────

Driftwood Santas

Materials
Driftwood, acrylic paints, paint-brush, fine-tipped permanent markers, clear acrylic spray

1. Rinse the sand and grit off the driftwood pieces and allow them to dry.

2. Paint the pieces to look like Santas, either as faces or as whole figures.

3. When the paint is dry, spray them with clear acrylic.

1. Soak the shells in a solution of one part bleach to three parts water for two or three days. Allow to dry.
2. If you have a power drill, drill a hole through the end of the shell.
3. Paint the shell the color of your choice. If the shell is particularly attractive, don't paint it. Rather, brush on a clear acrylic base containing glitter. Allow to dry.
4. To make a halo, form a loop in one end of the brass wire.
5. For a hanger, shape the monofilament into a loop. Thread both ends of the monofilament and the straight end of the brass wire through the bead cap, then through the bead.
6. Insert the wire and mono-filament into the hole in the shell. Working from underneath the shell, apply a large dollop of hot glue to hold the assembly in place.

   If you didn't drill a hole in the shell, hot-glue the head unit and the hanger to the back of the shell.
7. Untwist the paper ribbon and tie a piece of monofilament around the center, to shape it into wings. Hot-glue the wings to the back of the angel.
8. Place the center of the pearl garland in front of the angel's "neck." Wrap the ends around the neck and back to the front, to make the arms. Glue the arms to the front of the shell with tiny dabs of tacky glue. You may need to hold the garland in position until it dries a bit.
9. If desired, use tacky glue to attach a tiny shell between the angel's hands.

❋ SHELL ANGELS ❋

The iridescent wings of these angels shimmer in the tree lights.

Materials

Shells, household bleach, power drill with 1/16-inch (1.5 mm) bit, acrylic paint or clear acrylic base with glitter, paintbrush, 5-inch (13 cm) length of brass wire, monofilament, white "pearl" bead 3/4 inch (2 cm) in diameter, matching bead cap, 4-inch (10 cm) length of iridescent paper ribbon, 3-inch (8 cm) length of pearl garland, tiny flat shell (optional), glue gun, tacky glue

❈ SEASHELL TABLE TREE ❈

Finally: a way to use up all those shells you picked up at the beach three years ago. Besides, even the bathroom should have a Christmas tree.

Materials

Foam or paper cone 14 inches (35 cm) tall, low-melt glue gun, seashells, bath beads and hearts, narrow gold metallic ribbon, fine-gauge floral wire, narrow pink cord

1. Glue the shells onto the cone, covering it completely. Inset the bath beads and hearts as you go along.
2. To make a base, select a fairly flat shell large enough to hold the tree. Stabilize the large shell by hot-gluing small shells to the bottom of it where necessary to hold it level.
3. Glue the tree to the shell base.
4. Cut five lengths of the pink cord about 13 inches (33 cm) long and hot-glue their ends to the top of the tree. Allow the streamers to hang down the tree on all sides.
5. Make two bows from the gold metallic ribbon, wiring each one around the center to hold it together. Glue one bow on top of the tree and one at the base.

※ Agate Slices ※

If you've ever admired the rich colors and gorgeous patterns of agate, think Christmas; to become a tree ornament, an agate slice needs only a hanger. The inexpensive slices are available at stores that sell minerals, jewelry supplies, nature products, or even a wide range of gifts. Since agate is fairly heavy, select the smaller slices.

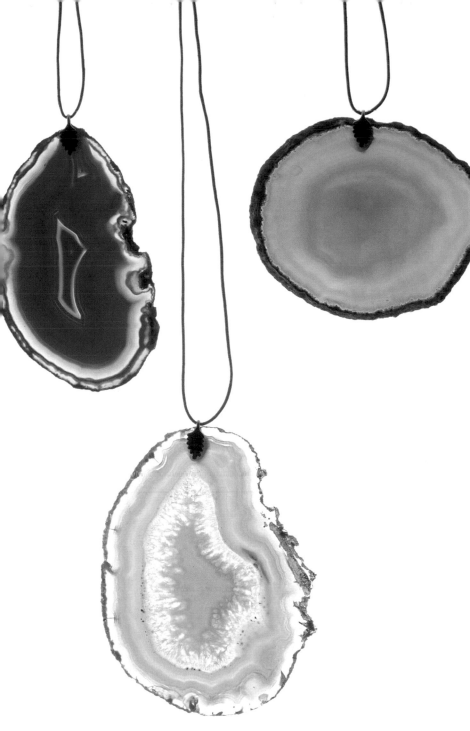

Materials
Agate slice, metal "feather" clasp, quick-setting epoxy, decorative cord

1. Wash and dry the agate, removing any glue left by price tags.
2. Bend a feather clasp into a U shape by bending it around a pencil, so that you get a smooth, round curve rather than an unpredictable kink.
3. Insert the edge of the agate slice into the hanger and use needle-nosed pliers to squeeze the clasp closed until both ends fit snugly against the agate. Remove the clasp from the agate.
4. Mix the two parts of the epoxy, following the manufacturer's instructions. Dab epoxy on both the agate and the clasp, where the two will meet, and insert the agate into the clasp. If there are any huge dollops of epoxy showing, try to wipe them off. Allow the epoxy to set.
5. Thread a loop of decorative cord though the hanger; gold-dyed leather cord is shown in the photo.

3. Continue in this fashion until the ball is covered with shavings.
4. To make a hanger, tie the cord in a loop and glue it to the ball.

———— ✄ ————

Hanging Beads

Materials
Round, unfinished, wooden beads in 3 sizes, beads resembling children's blocks, acrylic paints in primary colors, paintbrush, heavy jute cord or yarn

1. Paint the beads with the acrylic paints, mixing the sizes and colors. Allow to dry.
2. String the beads on the jute cord. Knot the cord below the bottom bead and above the top bead, leaving a tail to tie to the tree.

———— ✄ ————

Bead Garland

Materials
Oval, unfinished, wooden beads, black-and-white melon-shaped beads, red acrylic paint, paintbrush, jute cord or yarn

1. Paint the oval beads red and allow them to dry.
2. String the beads onto the jute cord, alternating the two types.
3. Knot the cord next to each end bead, leaving tails of cord on each end to tie to the tree.

———— ✄ ————

A Is for Apple

Materials
Unfinished plywood letters, numbers, and apple, acrylic paints in primary colors, paintbrush, jute cord or yarn, glue gun

1. Paint the letters with the acrylic paints and allow them to dry.
2. Form pieces of the cord or yarn into loops and hot-glue them to the back of the ornaments.

✄ CRAYONS AND PAINT ✄

For a child's room, make a tree filled with childish things: bundles of crayons tied up with yarn, ornaments of crayon shavings, painted wooden beads and blocks, and the letters and numbers that the child is learning. You might add a juicy, red apple.

Crayon Balls

Materials
Old crayons, crayon sharpener, paper plate, brush, white glue, foam ball 2-1/2 inches (6 cm) in diameter, decorative cord

1. Sharpen the crayons until you have lots of shavings. Place the shavings on a paper plate.
2. Brush white glue onto a section of the ball and roll the glued section in the shavings. Press more shavings on the ball with your hand if you need to.

Recycling Christmas Trees

In the United States alone, almost 40 million Christmas trees are cut each year. If they all came from one tree farm, it would be the size of Rhode Island. The average tree is six to seven feet (1.8 to 2.1 m) tall and weighs 15 to 20 pounds (7 to 9 kg).

That's a lot of landfill.

Fortunately, tree-recycling efforts are springing up just about everywhere. The most common municipal solution is to grind the trees into wood chips, then use them as mulch and soil amendments for erosion control and water retention.

More exotic uses include sinking the trees into a body of water to provide reefs for young fish and as bulwarks against beach erosion: the trees trap sand and thus help build dunes. They can even help restore wetlands. Strategically placed, they break up wave action and slow the flow of water, allowing a wetland the peace and quiet it needs to support a colony of plant life.

Subject Index

Project Index